Co-ordination Difficulties

Practical Ways Forward

Michèle G. Lee

Introduction by
Madeleine Portwood

David Fulton Publishers

David Fulton Publishers Ltd
The Chiswick Centre, 414 Chiswick High Road, London W4 5TF

www.fultonpublishers.co.uk

First published in Great Britain in 2004 by David Fulton Publishers
10 9 8 7 6 5 4 3 2 1

David Fulton Publishers is a division of ITV plc.

British Library Cataloguing in Publication Data
A catalogue record for this book is available from the British Library.

ISBN 1-84312-258-8

Designed and typeset by Kenneth Burnley, Wirral, Cheshire
Printed and bound in Great Britain

Contents

Preface

Working with children and adults with co-ordination difficulties is very rewarding and enjoyable. It is a condition that affects their whole lives, so all professionals need to work together in a holistic way to enable individuals to reach their maximum potential and develop the self-confidence and self-esteem required to become well-adjusted members of society.

The book provides detailed programmes of interaction for youngsters (aged 3–18) with co-ordination difficulties. Some of the chapters target specialist provision, i.e. for physiotherapy and occupational therapy, but there are also opportunities for teachers and assistants in mainstream settings to design and implement activities which will develop the skills of children with motor learning problems.

The Introduction and first chapter of the book were written by Madeleine Portwood, an educational psychologist who has specialised in dyspraxia and associated difficulties for many years and who is well known in her field. She provides an educational slant to the definition and theory. The following chapters consider therapy intervention which I have found valuable in my work. The section on standardised assessments was compiled by Lois Addy, an occupational therapist who has an in-depth knowledge in the field. The section on the assessment and treatment of fine motor skills and handwriting skills was written by Sheena Anderson, also an occupational therapist, who has spent many years working with children with dyspraxia and co-ordination difficulties. Finally, the last chapter considers the evidence from British therapists on the effectiveness of treatment and Appendix 4 provides a case study.

I hope that this book will prove a useful resource for those working with children who have co-ordination difficulties. I believe it will give them the encouragement to explore further the field of dyspraxia and to develop their own experience and understanding of the condition.

Acknowledgements

I would like to thank Jenny French (chartered physiotherapist) for all her hard work in assisting me with the original manuscript.

In particular, I would like to thank Madeleine Portwood for her contributions and especially for all her support and advice. In addition, occupational therapists Lois Addy and Sheena Anderson have provided important contributions and help.

For their support and assistance in writing this book, I would also like to thank: my husband, Nicholas Lee, for the photographs; Ivor Ganley and Lizzie Walsh for proof-reading; and Bernadette Mohan for assisting with the typing.

Finally, my special thanks go to my sons, Thomas and Alex, for being the models in the photographs.

Michèle G. Lee

Introduction

> Movement is a child's first language – it is the first medium of expansion of the physical and emotional conditions of an individual. Self-control begins with the control of movement (Kiphard and Schilling 1974).

I have spent the last 20 years working with children who have learning difficulties. During this time, it has become evident that patterns of early development signal future learning outcomes. Children who struggle to co-ordinate their movements, avoid inset puzzles and find dressing impossible often have problems with concentration, language development and relationships with their peers. Some of these children are described as autistic, dyslexic, dyspraxic or delinquent: virtually all have problems with co-ordination.

It is my intention to provide an overview of the co-occurrence of neurodevelopmental disorders in children and explain how the development of physical skills in the early years can improve the outcomes for many. Health and education practitioners have raised concerns over increasing numbers of children who have problems with concentration, co-ordination and learning. Before attaching diagnostic labels, however, it is important to consider why this might be the case.

The co-occurrence of dyslexia, dyspraxia and attention deficit/attention deficit hyperactivity disorder (ADD/ADHD) is well documented (Kaplan *et al.* 1998; Wimmer *et al.* 1998; Portwood 1999; Ramus *et al.* 2003). The College of Occupational Therapists, National Association of Paediatric Occupational Therapists (2003) concludes that children with co-ordination difficulties commonly have ADHD, dyslexia and speech and language impairments. Denckla *et al.* (1985) reported that dyslexic children were less competent than controls in tests relating to speed of movement, balance and co-ordination. Wolff (1999) identifies an association between impaired motor skills and language delay – 90 per cent of the dyslexic children with co-ordination difficulties also had motor-speech deficits. Many children with generalised learning difficulties have problems with co-ordination (Silver 1992). In addition, researchers have also identified autistic features, anxiety and depression co-occurring with co-ordination difficulties.

I have recently concluded a screening of more than 500 three-year-old children in pre-school settings in County Durham. In the study, 65 per cent of these pupils did not achieve the expected levels of competency in the development of motor skills. This is probably the result of changes in lifestyle. There are other 'distractions' that directly influence the time children spend developing their physical skills. Parents concerned about their children's safety restrict their movements beyond the boundaries of the home. Computers, 'Play Station' games and television schemes are the usual choices of many youngsters. This lack of opportunity to develop motor skills does account, in part, for the increases in children with co-ordination difficulties. For many of these pupils, a structured nursery/school-based programme focusing on the development of physical skills is sufficient. A significant proportion of young people, however, require the involvement of a specialist to complete a comprehensive assessment of skills to target particular areas of development. This is the focus of later chapters.

Educationalists are aware that the development of motor skills appears to have a direct effect on future learning outcomes. Goddard-Blyth and Hyland (1998) highlighted significant differences in the early development of groups of seven- to eight-year-old children with reading, writing and copying difficulties when compared with 'matched' controls. The children with 'difficulties' had a cluster of factors in acquisition of motor skills. They learned to walk later and many did not crawl. The development of language skills was delayed and co-ordinated activities such as riding a bike or catching a ball was problematic. They struggled to complete fine-motor tasks, fastening buttons and shoelaces. The researchers concluded that the discrepancy between the two groups increased over time. Delays in the development of motor skills impacted upon learning, which in itself was dependent upon the motor system for expression, reading, writing and copying.

The child must progress through a series of developmental stages as s/he learns to stand and balance independently. Children who have poorly developed postural control have difficulty sitting still and focusing their attention. They constantly adjust their position and exhibit a range of behaviours commonly associated with ADHD. These skills must be learned: the brain, through trial and error maintains control over balance, posture and involuntary movement (Kohen-Raz 1986).

There is growing concern among parents and teachers who are faced with increasing numbers of 'hyperactive' children, many of whom have problems with co-ordination. 'We can no longer leave this learning to the osmosis approach in which children select their own play and, as a consequence, their own learning' (Wetton 1997). Improving co-ordination should therefore have a direct impact on learning. This book has been produced to address these concerns and provide a structured scheme of physical therapy for children in which directed activities are targeted following a detailed assessment of skills.

Madeleine Portwood

Chapter 1

Understanding the Problem

Defining the focal group

An increasing number of children have problems planning and executing tasks with a motor-skill component. They are described variously as having: 'perceptual motor dysfunction', 'sensory integrative dysfunction', 'deficits in attention, motor control and perception (DAMP)', 'developmental dyspraxia', 'clumsy child syndrome' (Missiuna and Polatajko 1995). Although the condition was first recognised in the early 1900s, increasing awareness has provided evidence that demonstrates prevalence in 5 per cent of primary-aged schoolchildren (Gubbay 1975b; Henderson and Hall 1982; Sugden and Chambers 1998; Kadesjo and Gillberg 2001). This prompted recognition by the American Psychiatric Association (1994) and the World Health Organisation of a distinct movement-skill syndrome classified as developmental co-ordination disorder (DCD). At an international consensus meeting held to debate these different labels, the definition of DCD was accepted by researchers and clinicians (Polatajko *et al.* 1995).

Diagnostic features of DCD (adapted from American Psychiatric Association 1994, 315.4)

The essential feature of DCD is a marked impairment in the development of motor co-ordination (criterion A). The diagnosis is made only if this impairment significantly interferes with academic achievement or activities of daily living (criterion B). The diagnosis is made if the co-ordination difficulties are not due to a general medical condition (e.g. cerebral palsy, hemiplegia or muscular dystrophy) and the criteria are not met for pervasive developmental disorder (criterion C). If mental retardation is present, the motor difficulties are in excess of those usually associated with it (criterion D). The manifestations of this disorder vary with age and development. For example, younger children may display clumsiness and delays in achieving development motor milestones (e.g. walking, crawling, sitting, tying shoelaces, buttoning shirts, zipping trousers). Older children may display difficulties with the motor aspects of assembling puzzles, building models, playing ball and printing or writing.

Associated features and disorders

Problems commonly associated with DCD include delays in other non-motor milestones; associated disorders may include phonological disorder and expressive language disorder. Prevalence of DCD has been estimated to be as high as 6 per cent for children in the age range 5–11 years. Recognition of DCD usually occurs when the child first attempts such tasks as running, holding a knife and fork, buttoning clothes, or playing ball games. Its progression is variable. In some cases, lack of co-ordination continues through adolescence and adulthood.

Differential diagnosis

DCD must be distinguished from motor impairments that are due to a general medical condition. Problems in co-ordination may be associated with specific neurological disorders (e.g. cerebral palsy, progressive lesions of the cerebellum), but in these cases there is definite neural damage and abnormal findings on neurological examination. If mental retardation is present, DCD can be diagnosed only if the motor difficulties are in excess of those usually associated with the mental retardation. A diagnosis of DCD is not given if the criteria are met for a pervasive developmental disorder. Individuals with ADHD may fall, bump into things or knock things over, but this is usually due to distractibility and impulsiveness rather than to a motor impairment. If criteria for both disorders are met, both diagnoses can be given.

Summary of diagnostic criteria for DCD

A. Performance in daily activities that require motor co-ordination is substantially below that expected given the person's chronological age and measured intelligence. This may be manifested by marked delays in achieving motor milestones (e.g. walking, crawling, sitting), dropping things, 'clumsiness', poor performance in sports or poor handwriting.
B. The disturbance in criterion A significantly interferes with academic achievement or activities of daily living.
C. The disturbance is not due to a general medical condition (e.g. cerebral palsy, hemiplegia or muscular dystrophy) and does not meet criteria for a pervasive developmental disorder.
D. If mental retardation is present, the motor difficulties are in excess of those usually associated with it.

Even with reference to DSM-IV (American Psychiatric Association 1994), however, the literature describing DCD includes wide-ranging terminology and criteria. Sugden and Keogh (1990) found that the characteristics of children diagnosed with DCD depended upon the source of referral, the professional background of the assessor and the type of assessment used.

Interpretation of the literature on DCD is further compounded by the lack of inclusion criteria. Geuze *et al.* (2001) reviewed 164 publications on the study of DCD and found that only 60 per cent were based on objective criteria as there is no 'generally accepted' level of motor proficiency to define clumsiness (Sugden and Keogh 1990). As a result, they recommended that a child scoring below the 15th percentile on standardised tests of motor skill (Henderson 1992: Sugden Movement ABC) and having an IQ score above 69 (Wechsler Intelligence Scales) would qualify for a diagnosis of DCD. For some children, a 'diagnosis' provided access to support services, often with additional funding. Standardised assessments are the focus of discussion in Chapter 3.

The treatment programmes described in Chapter 4 have been shown to benefit children with co-ordination difficulties, even when DCD is not the primary diagnosis. Improving co-ordination can relate directly to improvements in learning (Myers 2002).

Movement and learning

Developmental disorders of childhood are usually attributed to some 'brain-related' event (Portwood 2000). The brain controls the reaction of the body to the environment. The building block of the brain's structure is the neurone. These neurones (numbering approximately 10 billion) actively make and break connections with one another to form a neural network that becomes increasingly more complex. This forms the central nervous system, which is divided into two parts:

1. The brain stem and limbic system interpret signals from within the body. They are connected to the systems responsible for regulating heartbeat, respiration and digestion.
2. The thalamo-cortical system, which interprets signals external to the body: sight, sound, taste, smell and the body's awareness of its position in space. Higher brain function is located in the cortex.

Five weeks after conception, cells specialise to form the nervous system. The most significant aspect of brain development occurs after 30 weeks' gestation and continues through the first few years of life. This is a critical period of child development during which the nerve cells form the majority of their interconnections. Intellectual ability is not determined by the number of neurones but the number of connecting links between them, which are directly affected by the messages the brain receives from the environment.

Esther Thelen, a developmental psychologist at the University of Indiana, completed a study of babies and produced evidence that at a very young age, the child begins to select behaviours that will become the building blocks for later development (Thelen 1989). Shortly after birth, a baby learns to fixate on an object and by two months he begins to make anticipatory movements towards the object with a closed fist, but at this early stage in life he is unable to co-ordinate and plan movements. As part of her study, Thelen attached motion sensors to the limbs of babies in order that their movements could be recorded. Analysis of this information provided insight as to the acquisition of basic skills. At six months, the child's movement becomes more purposeful and directed; reaching and grasping becomes automatic. Previously it had been thought that these skills were somehow genetically programmed, but this research confirmed that the child must learn to plan for himself the sequence of movements required to perform intentional actions. He is able to select from a range of random movements those that work and over time these movements are 'programmed' and become automatic.

The neural pathways that produce purposeful behaviour are reinforced. Gerald Edelman (1989) suggested that such connections are formed due to a process of natural selection. As the connections between nerve cells increase, signals will travel more quickly through the network. For the brain to function efficiently, it is important that information transfers easily between the limbic and cortical systems. The development of movement skills improves this efficiency and consequently, where co-ordination difficulties are evident, there is an increased likelihood that the child will have specific learning problems.

Developing early movement skills

Children progress through a series of developmental stages and it is important that they access opportunities to extend movement skills. In the early years, balance and co-ordination is achieved through a process of trial and error. There is increasing awareness of speed and distance; a child taking his first independent steps without support realises that the only means of maintaining an upright position is to move at speed. When the motion decreases, balance is more dependent upon postural control.

Young children who have not acquired the skills naturally to use their limbs to counterbalance their body effectively can benefit from accessing a structured motor programme in the home playgroup or nursery. The checklist of movement skills provides details of the expected level of skill acquisition.

Movement checklist 0–12 months

- Turns head from side to side when placed on front or back
- Visually tracks object from side to side
- When placed on back, makes random movements with arms and legs
- When placed on front, raises head and then chest from floor
- Makes purposeful movements towards object secured in line of vision
- Brings hands together in midline
- Fingers extended from grasping reflex
- When placed on front, is able to press down with hands and raise chest from floor
- Attempts to roll from side to side
- In supported sitting position, is able to rotate head and upper body
- Reaches and grasps objects with hands
- Rolls from front to back and reverse
- Places foot (flat) on floor and 'stands' with total adult support
- Sits unsupported (shows saving reflexes)
- Pivots in sitting position and moves freely to knees
- Crawls on all fours
- Holds upright kneeling
- Pushes from kneeling to standing position with support
- Still standing with support, transfers weight between feet
- Begins to cruise round the furniture
- Walks with adult support, both hands held or pushing toy
- Moves from a standing to sitting position

(Source: adapted from Portwood 2003)

Movement checklist 12–24 months

- Stands independently leaning against adult or furniture
- Picks up small objects, fingers and thumb in opposition
- Removes objects from peg board or handled inset puzzle
- Walks with one hand held
- Sits on floor (legs 'V-shaped') and rolls ball away from self
- Takes a few independent steps
- Stands alone
- Crawls up stairs
- Places one 2-inch block on top of another
- Makes 'scribble' marks on paper
- Develops hand preference
- Marks on paper of same direction (across, up, down)
- Completes single piece form board
- Separates screw toys
- Bends over to pick up objects without falling over
- Copies circular scribble
- Throws a ball
- Uses preferred hand most of the time
- Walks backwards safely

(Source: adapted from Portwood 2003)

Movement checklist 24–36 months

Gross motor skills

- Crawling through a tunnel (2m length) co-ordinating arms and legs appropriately
- Walking backwards, forwards and sideways, arms alongside the body
- Running a distance of 10m without tripping or falling over
- Jumping from a low step or on the spot with feet together
- Climbing up and down stairs in an adult fashion, placing one foot on each step
- Walking heel/toe along a measured distance of 3m
- Balancing along a bench/plank raised (10cm) from the floor
- Balancing on either foot for 5+ seconds

Fine motor skills

- Established hand preference
- Building a tower of 6+ (2.5cm) bricks
- Reassemble a screw toy or remove the top from a jar or bottle
- Thread a determined sequence of large beads, e.g. two red, one blue, two yellow
- Complete 6-piece inset puzzle/jigsaw
- Copy simple shapes, e.g. line, cross, circle, square

(Source: adapted from Portwood 2003)

Children in primary and secondary education identified as having DCD, dyslexia or ADHD usually show evidence of difficulty by the age of 3. Low-level intervention at this stage can have a significant effect on future learning. Children with co-ordination difficulties are likely to have:

- reduced visual motor sensitivity;
- unsteady visual perception; and
- reduced sensitivity to changes in sound frequency.

This in turn will affect their ability to

- Judge speed
  - How fast they are travelling in relation to objects and people in the space around them.
  - How quickly a ball, for example, is travelling towards them.
- Judge distances
  - How far away the ground might be when they jump from the top of a climbing frame.
  - How to plan movements to jump in and out of hoops.
  - How to throw and kick accurately at targets.
  - How to move safely between objects without bumping into them or falling.
- Focus on the task
  - Convergence difficulties may result in 'double vision' making it more difficult to plan where the body or object might be.
- Respond to verbal instructions quickly
  - The class is given the instruction to change direction: everyone else turns, the dyslexic child does not.
  - Sequencing sounds/rhythms to movements such as taking an active part in marching or performing actions in response to a beat.

Intervention

Programmes should include activities that will focus and develop these particular skills. For a number of children, their co-ordination difficulties are the result of limited opportunity to practise skills and they will improve very quickly. In the early years it is very important that the children do not feel singled out and different from the rest of the group. Find activities suitable for the whole class to join in, but remember to:

- Keep the use of language to a minimum.
- Always demonstrate the task yourself or ask a child who is competent in the skill.
- Use visual cues such as coloured spots or markers – don't say 'Find a space'.
- Break down the task into small achievable targets.
- Make sure that each skill is learned separately before using them in combinations – the child must be able to balance (both feet flat on the floor) and then on each leg (5+ seconds) before hopping and skipping as these skills are acquired separately.

It is important that the health and education services available to children are co-ordinated. Educationalists can provide school-based programmes specifically targeting those children with less-complex difficulties. Many children, however, require access to specialist services, which can be offered in a clinic, school or home.

Chapter 2

Referral

Introduction

The initial concern about a child may originate from a number of sources such as the classroom teacher, the parents, health visitor or GP. Generally speaking, however, there are two main sources of referrals:

Health:	via the GP after parents or health visitors express concern;
Education:	via the school doctor or educational psychologist after concern has been expressed by the class teacher.

There are specific ages when most referrals take place.

Five years old

This is the first time that many parents are likely to have an opportunity to compare their child to other children of similar age. In addition, the class teacher will know what to expect children of this age group to achieve. The implementation of the baseline assessments for all children entering school also has an impact on referrals at this age.

Seven years old

Some children may have appeared to have coped initially or it may have been decided to give the child time to mature. At this age, however, any difficulties the child is experiencing become more apparent, e.g. dressing and changing for PE and games, messy eating, drawing difficulties and fine and gross motor skills. In addition, the child may show a number of difficulties with games and in the more structured school environment; organisational difficulties may be evident.

Eleven years old

Children who have struggled but overcome their difficulties throughout the junior school may encounter significant problems with the change of pace and organisational skills that are required for secondary education. Lack of confidence and the feeling of being different add to the problems. Some youngsters develop very good coping strategies but many experience emotional and psychological difficulties and may require psychological support.

The team approach

The improved awareness of dyspraxia and DCD has led to better identification and treatment as well as a growth in the number of skilled individuals. It is imperative that all those working with the child and family share information from assessment and compare progress in order to identify the outcomes of intervention. Key workers have an important role to play within the team as they will provide regular input and be responsible for communicating information between the team, the child and the family. They are also responsible for informing the school and the GP of changes occurring and of progress made. It is important that all team members understand and respect each other's roles so that active skill-sharing can enhance teamwork (French and Patterson 1992).

Parental reporting

Parents often describe the child's problems quite differently from teachers or therapists – they may be very concerned with the child's learning and behavioural difficulties but may not link these to his co-ordination or perceptual problems. Some parents may have noticed that their child is not competing well with his peers or siblings or reaching the same goals as his classmates. It is important to listen to parents. In many cases, parents have voiced their concerns for some time before receiving appropriate help. They may have been told that there is nothing wrong with their child or that 'he is just lazy and could do better' – some parents are even told that it is their fault and that their child's problems are due to poor parenting skills (Dyspraxia Foundation 1997)!

The problems often reported by parents may include the following:

Unhappy at school

- lack of educational progress
- concern expressed by teacher

Behaviour problems

- clinging
- no friends
- tantrums or easily loses temper
- gives up and refuses to try activities

Poor writing

- poor style so unable to read it or writing is not joined
- poor speed and cannot keep up with class

Falls over a lot

- never looks where he is going
- lots of bruises
- knocks into objects
- is easily knocked over in the playground
- slips and falls when on climbing frames and has difficulty knowing how to climb on and off furniture/climbing frame

Difficulty appreciating the distance between himself and others

- bumps into doorways/furniture
- tendency to stand very close to another person

Messy eater

- tendency to use fingers
- has difficulty cutting food with a knife
- has food all over face and clothes

- spills food off the plate
- knocks over and spills drinks
- drops plate when carrying it

Difficulty with dressing/undressing

- once completed looks a mess (like 'Just William')
- cannot tie shoelaces
- has difficulty fastening buttons
- unable to remember correct sequence of putting on clothes
- is very slow
- does not know which way round the clothes should go (i.e. clothes are put on back to front)

Frequently late in learning to (or cannot) ride a bicycle

- poor balance
- has difficulty knowing how to use pedals
- cannot use brakes to stop bicycle
- unable to steer or turn

Difficulty remembering instructions

- has difficulty following instructions when asked
- has difficulty with copying from the board
- has difficulty copying instructions when shown (e.g. in science)

Poor concentration

- is easily distracted
- cannot stay on task for long

Poor self-organisational skills

- generally reported to be disorganised and has no order for where to place personal items such as toys and clothes
- room very untidy
- has difficulty remembering what items to take to school, those required for homework and items to be taken home
- cannot plan which things are needed for a specific activity (e.g. items required for swimming lessons)

When questioned, parents may well reveal that the child encountered difficulties from an early age. In some cases, parents will report that the child was slow to reach his milestones. Most therapists are familiar with the recognised ages for reaching milestones but it should also be remembered that this does not just include rolling, sitting, crawling, standing and walking – many children are also late in walking up and down stairs reciprocally, jumping, hopping and skipping. In addition, they may have been poor feeders and unsettled babies. Lee and Gronmark (2000) carried out an audit of 110 children from their practice focusing specifically on the ages at which children diagnosed with dyspraxia had reached their milestones. From their study, the majority of children had reached their early milestones (sitting and crawling) at age-appropriate stages, but 40 per cent had been delayed in standing and 30 per cent in walking; only 30 per cent of the children had never crawled. More significantly, parents reported that their children could not skip, had difficulty with jumping and had always been poor at ball skills. This would suggest that it is the later skills which become more noticeably delayed.

Sheridan (1997) stated that a child should be able to reach the following milestones at the stated times:

- Ride a tricycle using pedals by the age of three years and be an expert rider by the age of four.
- Throw a ball overhand and catch a large ball on or between extended arms by the age of three years and by four years of age be able to use a bat.
- Kick a ball forcibly by the age of three years.
- Jump from the bottom step of the stairs at two years.
- Walk up and down stairs reciprocally (but holding onto a rail) by the age of four years.
- Hop on one foot by the age of four years and by the age of five hop 2–3m.
- Skip by the age of five.
- Dress and undress alone by the age of four except for laces, ties and back buttons which can be achieved from five years onwards.

Parents accept their child's problems in different ways: they may deny that a problem exists; they may be frustrated that no one else recognises the problems; they may react with tolerance and understanding. There may be many reasons for these acceptance differences. Parents may not want their child to be identified as being 'different' and they certainly do not want him 'picked out' in the classroom situation to add embarrassment to his problems. Some parents also have very high expectations of their children and this in turn can place stress on the child, adding to his difficulties. In some cases, parents may have experienced similar difficulties themselves as children and will welcome help to ensure that their child does not suffer the same difficulties as they did.

Parents have a great deal of information to give to the therapist, e.g. birth history, the child's behaviour, their own attitude to their child's problems. I have found that a pre-assessment questionnaire for the parents to complete is a very useful tool. It enables parents to express in writing how they view the situation and to answer questions which they may have difficulty answering in front of their child. It is also useful to have a section for the school to complete. Some simple questions and activities (such as drawing a picture of a person) may be asked of the child in order to save time during the assessment. In my work, the questionnaire as devised by Lee and Smith (1998) has proved successful and parents have reported that it was simple to complete (see Appendix 2 for an example of a questionnaire set for children to complete).

Reporting by teachers

The teacher may have noted similar areas of difficulty to the parents or they may have a completely different picture of the child.

Teachers often report that the child has:

Poor concentration and is easily distracted

- constantly looking around classroom/out of window or watching other children in the classroom
- unable to focus on one task for longer than a few minutes

Poor writing ability

- poor pencil grip
- poor style of writing; badly formed letters, not anchored on a line, illegible and slow

Poor at PE and apparatus

- difficulty throwing and catching balls
- difficulty kicking balls
- difficulty climbing on and off apparatus
- difficulty following instructions
- slow runner and cannot carry out skills such as hopping and skipping
- poor at participating in games and activities
- difficulty with, and slowness of, changing for games

Few friends

- spends break times alone
- does not appear to understand about taking turns and sharing
- has difficulty understanding when it is appropriate to speak or interrupt a conversation

Naughty or disruptive in class

- 'acts the fool' – perhaps to get out of an activity which they find hard or in order to make peers laugh which they see as a positive step to making friends
- does not appear to listen to or follow instructions

Unable to sit still

- moves around the classroom

Difficulty remembering instructions when shown or asked

- following instructions in classroom
- copying from the board
- copying from text

Generally poor organisational skills

- difficulty planning essays or activities
- difficulty getting equipment ready for each lesson
- does not have the right books ready for the correct class
- messy presentation of work and not in a logical format
- generally untidy

Liaison with the school

It is very important that the teacher understands the nature of the child's difficulties and the help which is available. The teacher may not have come across a child with such problems before and will welcome advice and help for the classroom and PE settings. The way in which the child is treated in the classroom affects how well he is able to cope with his problems and therefore close liaison with the teacher is very important. It is often hard due to lack of resources and time to provide the school with good liaison but offering advisory leaflets and sending summaries of the report will help. In addition, I have found that asking parents, teacher and therapist to complete a liaison diary is a useful method of ensuring that the child's progress is monitored. It also provides feedback of any changes.

Therapists need an understanding of their role within education if their skills are to be recognised. Informing teachers of the condition and its associated difficulties is important, and offering advice that can be implemented both in the classroom and in games lessons is vital (this will be discussed later).

Chapter 3

Assessment

Normal development

In order to assess a child with a disability, it is important first to understand the process of normal development. The development of organised movement begins before birth and rapidly improves as myelination and dendritic interconnections occur. A child has first to interpret adequately sensory input before being able to make a motor response. Children learn from these movement experiences: the developmental building blocks of learning stack one upon another and the child develops a repertoire of different skills. Some examples of normal development were given in Chapter 2 (for more in-depth information see the published sources on this subject).

The importance of self-esteem and self-confidence

Motor development influences intellectual, social and emotional development. Through play, a child will practise and perfect movements and activities until he becomes proficient. Exploration of the environment leads to knowledge about the child's world and the ability to judge distances between himself and other objects. In addition, the child learns the formulation of basic concepts, e.g. under/over, up/down, which will later be used in learning basic academic skills.

Early developmental milestones may be delayed, thus limiting a child's mobility and capacity to explore. Perceptual skills such as knowing the depth or height of a step or kerb may be deficient. Touch and texture are learnt primarily from experiencing the sensation through the sensory receptors; if this is limited delays may occur.

Social and emotional development occurs through interaction with others by gesture, play and speech. From this, self-concept and self-confidence develop (French and Patterson 1992). A child who has confidence in movement will develop a good self-image: he will attempt new tasks and explore new areas without being threatened with failure which in turn results in a loss of confidence and a hampering of the learning progress. The child with dyspraxia, however, will often have poor experiences of attempting new activities. This in turn will prevent him from wanting to attempt new activities for fear of further failure. More importantly, failure may lead to truancy and, in some cases, juvenile delinquency. Research in the US revealed that learning difficulties (including dyspraxia) were more prevalent in delinquent than non-delinquent groups (Lerner 1985; Hall 1995). It can be seen that movement is the basis for learning skills and with limited or with impaired movement skills, as in the case of the dyspraxic child, problems arise and escalate as the child grows older.

A child judges his motor performance by comparing his own skills with those of his peers. He may observe his peers attempting a new skill that he has not tried and will use his observations to attempt the task himself. In contrast, a child with dyspraxia will observe that his peers find it easier to achieve tasks and skills than he does. This in turn leads to a further decline in self-confidence and self-esteem.

The approval/disapproval of parents, carers and teachers also plays an important role in the development of a child's skills. Each will give a great deal of praise and positive encouragement to a child attempting a new skill, thereby boosting the child's confidence. This is an important element when dealing with children with dyspraxia. All those involved with the child must continue to be positive and provide lots of encouragement – it is all too easy to fall into the trap of making negative comments, e.g. 'Don't try that in case you fall as you always do!'

Early recognition

If problems with poor self-esteem and self-confidence are to be avoided then early recognition is of paramount importance. In some children, a diagnosis of dyspraxia is straightforward. For example, the child may not explore the environment, he may have poor stability, poor perceptual skills, a dislike of being moved and/or difficulty organising changes of position. An alternative profile may show the very active child who, in his early years, had feeding difficulties, flinched when touched or cried easily when being dressed. Obviously such an early diagnosis must exclude differential diagnosis and should be the findings of a 'team' and not the diagnosis of one team member in isolation.

Many pre-school children, however, are much more difficult to identify accurately. They may appear to be just a little slow in their development and parents may not have been able to compare their progress with siblings or other children of the same age. It may not be until they start school that difficulties in playing and learning become apparent and concerns are raised. Parents are not usually taught how to handle their children or how to recognise abnormalities in behaviour or movement. They do, however, often *know* that something is amiss. It is very possible that some of the early difficulties which children experience may be due to slow but normal maturation or restricted environment, i.e. no exposure to playgrounds or other opportunities to experience gross motor challenges. Children with maturational delay, however, catch up very quickly in their first year at nursery or school.

Early referral enables early evaluation and intervention. Although several tests do exist, very few are designed in such a way as to cover all the aspects that therapists and teachers need to assess. Therapists and psychologists usually find that they need to use additional tests and clinical observations alongside their chosen standardised test. Children with specific learning difficulties will require further referral for more specific diagnostic testing and for educational assessment.

Screening

Normal development is very varied and depends on environmental, cultural and genetic factors. In general, children's development is very diverse and it is known that there is not only one pattern of characteristics that identifies the child with dyspraxia but a whole range of characteristics that may or may not affect each child to a differing degree. The importance of screening is to identify affected children as early as possible. Most screening procedures have pass/fail criteria with a grey borderline category of 'at risk' children.

Observation by an experienced health professional or teacher is by far the quickest and easiest way to identify a child who is functioning significantly differently from other children in a similar group. Observational screening by health visitors, school nurses and therapists may identify children with motor difficulties, but may not always pick up children with more subtle difficulties. Failure in the classroom is often the first indicator that a child may have a motor learning problem. School doctors may not see the child until he is referred by the teacher or the therapist. Therapists are frequently being asked to undertake training in school to help teachers and school doctors identify these children.

Many tests are available for health professionals but very few have been standardised for use on children in Britain (Gubbay 1975a). Therapists have tended to use their own selection of test items from the existing batteries of tests they find most useful and reliable (e.g. equilibrium reactions, bilateral tasks, diado-kokinesis, Romberg, Fog, Schilder, tapping, draw a man, etc.). These will identify many children with obvious motor-learning problems. Many therapists and medical officers, however, agree that some children are not identified until six, seven or eight years of age when they either have to cope with a more organised school structure or are unable any longer to 'avoid' tasks which they find difficult.

Infant school

At this age, parents may often voice concern that their child shows a marked difference in ability from the other children who are starting school. Some difficulties may now become more noticeable: messy eating, dressing problems, drawing difficulties and fine and gross motor skills. The introduction of baseline assessments for all children entering reception class has ensured that more children are identified at an earlier age than was previously possible.

Junior school

The child's problems are increasingly evident at this age and teachers often refer the child for a fuller assessment of his special needs. The codes of practice enable a formal process to take place to ensure that difficulties are highlighted and that the correct provision is made for each child. If the child's poor academic progress is due to a significant motor-learning problem, co-operation in the planning of suitable intervention is essential between the class teacher and therapist. In some cases, additional non-teaching assistants can help in carrying out programmes.

Secondary school

Even if the referral is late, it is important for an accurate assessment of the child's problems in conjunction with his educational assessment. Research has been carried out in order to determine the effects of therapy at this age. Lee and Smith (1998) showed that secondary schoolchildren receiving their treatment made just as much improvement as those in junior school. It is becoming more apparent (Portwood 2000) that the younger the child is treated the better – fewer behavioural difficulties are likely to develop. Those children who do not receive intervention by secondary school age have a higher incidence of delinquency in adolescence.

The assessment process

Initial observation

- Standardised/non-standardised assessments
- Clinical observations
- Parent interview
- Evaluation
- Report

The assessment

Initial observation

The assessment is usually the first contact the therapist will have with the child and his family. It is an important time, not just because it enables the therapist to determine the child's problems – it also allows a relationship to be established with the child and his parents for the future. It is imperative therefore that the child enjoys the session and that he is able to feel relaxed and comfortable in a non-threatening environment.

Assessment, in fact, should be ongoing as it can be very difficult to assess a child in one session. The child may not be able to concentrate for the length of time required and different areas of difficulty may not become apparent until later. It is important to observe the relationship between the child, parents and siblings and to identify the child's likes and dislikes as well as his strengths and weaknesses. A play environment is essential for observational assessment. An experienced eye and the ensuing discussion with the parents will bring to light some of the problems. During the first assessment, the therapist should ensure that the child feels relaxed and concentrate on building a rapport with the parents.

As in *all* assessment situations, emphasis is placed on the child's abilities. The therapist is looking to identify the child's strengths and reasons for difficulties – *not* to list *all* the tasks the child cannot do. Parents should be made welcome at the assessment: it will give them an opportunity to observe their child and understand the assessment and the reasons for the difficulties identified. Parents often find the assessment helpful and many have reported that it was not until the child was asked to perform a certain task that they realised he could not do it. This in turn enabled them to link, for example, the child's inability to ride his bike to his motor learning difficulty.

The therapist should assess not only motor function but also perceptual skills. Children learn to perceive sensory input relating to balance, postural control, body awareness in space and touch systems. Understanding concepts such as under/over, up/down, bigger/smaller, nearer/further are the basic building blocks of understanding shape and form. This enables them to learn about the environment in which they function. As the systems mature, self-esteem, confidence and personality develop (Silver 1991). Many therapists believe these aspects to be vital to assessment and will use additional test items to cover them (e.g. B/G Steem, see Appendix 1).

Gathering the facts

As previously stated, before assessment takes place it is important to gain as much information as possible from the parents, teachers and other professionals who have been involved with the child. This will give the therapist an indication of some of the problems and concerns. Questionnaires can be used for both parents and teachers prior to the assessment, thereby allowing concerns to be raised and questions to be asked which may otherwise prove embarrassing if answered in front of the child (Appendix 2). Simple questionnaires can also be given to the child beforehand so that his likes and dislikes are known (Appendix 2).

Considerations

The room should have:

- not too much equipment since this could distract the child
- all necessary equipment close at hand
- correct lighting and temperature, e.g. ensure the child will neither be blinded by direct sunlight nor find the room too dark
- a chair for the parent
- no distracting noises such as telephones or other sounds
- sufficient space to observe movement and gross motor skills

The therapist should:

- have been taught to assess and treat children with movement problems
- be relaxed and have time for the session
- not be interrupted and not taken out of the session for any reason
- have collected as many relevant facts as possible beforehand
- have ready all the paperwork needed beforehand
- give encouragement
- **ENSURE THAT THE CHILD ENJOYS THE ASSESSMENT AND IS NOT AWARE OF FAILURE**

Initial observation

The assessment process begins with the observation of the child in school, at home or in the clinic. The therapist will be watching the child's general performance, behaviour and level of activity. An explanation of the assessment process is crucial so that the parents understand what will take place during the assessment and how to prepare their child. Parents are often concerned about the outcome of assessment and may need to be reassured. Parents and children should be advised in advance how long the process may take and introduced to those team members who will be involved in the assessment.

The therapist may use recognised and standardised or non-standardised tests. It is recommended that additional clinical observations are used alongside standardised methods as in many cases the standardised tests do not give direction on which areas to treat.

Assessment is crucial. Many different groups of children, i.e. those with motor learning difficulties, basic co-ordination problems and children with learning disabilities, can be assessed using similar tools. There is often no one ideal testing tool, however, and the therapist may have to choose from several different tests in order to provide a precise assessment.

Assessment tests overview

Doctors do not, on the whole, use psychometric testing but rely on functional observational and descriptive tests (Bayley 1969; Griffiths 1970) to assess function of everyday tasks. These tests, which give a qualitative measure of how well the child performs certain tasks, are carried out by paediatricians to identify specific areas of neurological dysfunction. They may identify hard and soft neurological signs which may be interfering with the child's learning ability. Psychologists can provide psychometric testing and diagnostic testing.

Different types of measures available

Pre–post measures

This is a more traditional means of evaluative collection. It is a popular way of proving or disproving a theory or a programme's effectiveness. It is a quantitative means of data collection which can yield an enormous amount of information in a very economic way.

There are various means of pre–post test measuring:

- Standardised measures
- Criterion-referenced assessments
- Rated questionnaires

Standardised measures

These are scored assessments which have previously been validated using a large population and have proved to be reliable. The scores and norms are calculated through previous research. These standardised assessments are, on the whole, efficient, simple to use, require minimal effort to administer or undertake and are easy to score.

Examples of these are:

- Movement of ABC Battery
- Frostig Test of Visual Perception
- Index of Self-Esteem (ISE)
- Rivermead Perceptual Battery

These tests usually have a norm population scoring system and can give scaled and standard scores, percentile rank and even age equivalent. The standardised test can be used to score a client at the commencement and conclusion of a programme and comparisons can be drawn from the differences in the results.

Advantages of using standardised measures

- They have been *previously validated* and *prepared* so time is not taken to establish criteria or pilot a measure.
- They are usually easy to administer.
- They are easy to score.
- They are an effective means of proving/disproving theories.

Disadvantages of using standardised measures

- The measurement only meets the requirements of the original purpose; it may not meet the needs of the research proposed, limiting flexibility of use.
- Certain tests take a considerable time to administer, e.g. The Californian Sensory Integration test by Ayres.
- Certain tests may not be accessible to certain professionals.
- Some assessment batteries are very expensive.
- Some assessments have a time limitation on when they can be repeated and therefore may not suit the research time plan.
- When more than one assessment is required, administration may be time-consuming.
- The therapist may require training in order to administer the assessment.

Criterion-referenced assessments

These are valuable when a standardised assessment is not available to meet the *precise* needs of the research being tackled. In this case, the researcher designs his/her own scales and criteria to suit the research questions. A criterion-referenced measurement is concerned principally with the individual's ability to perform tasks representative of some specific criterion. It compares an individual's performance to an established criterion rather than to a population sample as in norm-referenced tests. A criterion-referenced test enables the planning of a therapeutic procedure because the information it provides outlines skill attainment and need.

Advantages of criterion-referenced assessments

- They are specific to the research proposed.
- They can be exceptionally detailed if required.
- They are easy to administer and score.
- They are economic and do not restrict professional use.

Disadvantages of criterion-referenced assessments

- They are quite difficult to clarify in the first instance and setting up can be time-consuming.
- There needs to be some piloting of scale to ensure reliability.
- They may be seen to be subjective.

Rated questionnaires

These have been discussed previously ('Gathering the facts' above).

Further reading

W. Dunn (1990) 'Establishing inter-rater reliability on a criterion-referenced development check list', *Occupational Therapy Journal of Research* **10**(6): 377–80.
J.K. Olson *et al.* (1991) 'Criterion-related validity', *Canadian Journal of Nursing Research* **23**: 49–59.
J. Ward (1971) 'On the concept of criterion-referenced measurement', *Journal of Educational Psychology* **40**: 314–33.

Rating the assessment

Following administration of the assessments, the test must then be scored. This can be done in three ways: (1) Researcher rated (2) Ipsative rating (3) Consensus rated.

Researcher rating

The evaluator scores the test using the previously written criterion scales at the beginning of the project and again at the end.

Ipsative rating

The individual participants in the research score themselves. This is especially appropriate where there is a need to measure pain, anxiety, guilt, etc. In this instance, there is a high face validity because they are measuring things that only they can report on thereby ensuring accuracy.

Consensus rating

This method requires a relative or colleague to score the item being researched; another member of staff or relative also scores. These are compared and a consensus agreed.

Standardised tests

A detailed list of standardised tests and their reliability can be found in Appendix 1. They can be used over a wide age range to assess various functions and can provide a useful basis for developing intervention programmes.

Clinical observations

Clinical observations, used by therapists to assess a child in a systematic way, are a recording method consisting of a checklist of tasks – the outcome of the observations will identify the child's problem areas. Accurate interpretation of the assessment is the key to appropriate intervention. If the outcome of the assessment is not conclusive then further testing will be required, either by the therapist or by another team member, e.g. if the child has visuo-perceptual problems, an orthoptist may be involved in the assessment. For those children whose poor co-ordination is a symptom of a more global delay, further neurological and psychometric testing may be needed.

The assessment may identify a concern over diagnosis, in which case a referral back to the paediatrician may be required. It should be borne in mind, however, that the child will still need to be treated. It is important for the therapist to always consider differential diagnosis, e.g. muscular dystrophy, cerebral palsy, etc.

Parent interview

Additional historical information provided by the parent/carer may reveal other underlying problems which the therapist has not identified. Expertise in parent interview techniques is developed with guidance and practice. Therapists unused to this form of assessment are strongly advised to seek supervision and advice from more experienced colleagues as the information collected can be vital to the accuracy of the assessment as a whole. A good relationship between the parents and the therapist is essential to ensure that parents do not regard the questions as intrusive. The use of open-ended questions will encourage the parents' responses and give additional information from the child's early days which will be invaluable to understanding the child's problems.

General assessment

The majority of activities require the use of a number of skills, therefore many tasks carried out in an assessment consist of skills of more than one type as the following example illustrates:

Task: Writing
Skills required: Shoulder control
Balance (pelvic control, active trunk flexion and extension)
Eye tracking
Eye/hand co-ordination
Muscle strength in hand
  tactile discrimination
  transitional finger movement
Perceptual, proprioceptive and kinaesthetic skills
Short-term visual and verbal memory
Midline crossing
Spatial awareness
Directional awareness
Motor planning
Attention ability
Confidence
Desire

Motor skills

It is well recognised that children with learning difficulties (whether severe, moderate, mild or specific) often have motor problems such as gross/fine motor co-ordination, more general motor planning or motor learning/perceptual skills.

The examples suggested are only a few of the many activities which may demonstrate these areas. Wherever possible, the therapist should use a score system so that measurements may be taken at the end of treatment to show the improvement in a particular area. Scores may be taken of the time in which a task is achieved or the number of tasks carried out in a specified time.

Muscle tone

A number of children with dyspraxia have low muscle tone. It is important to assess the full range of movement, hypermobility of any joints and general muscle strength (there is usually no relationship between muscle tone and muscle strength). Some children do have high tone and appear to move awkwardly while others may have fluctuating tone.

SHOULDER CONTROL

This relates to the muscle strength and joint laxity around the shoulder girdle. It is an important factor for hand functions and a prerequisite for the writing function.

Assessment	Considerations
A. Statically: In prone lying, bearing weight on forearms or extended arms and reach for objects	– is the head in midline? – is the weight through the forearms equal? – are the arms adducted or abducted? – is there propping or leaning? – consider the grasp when reaching – are the hips or knees flexed or adducted? – does the body weight shift considerably when reaching out?
B. Dynamically: Wheelbarrows, i.e. walking on the hands with the feet held at the ankles. The number of steps the child is able to achieve should be documented. Equal-sized steps should be taken with either hand. The hands should point forwards and not land heavily on the ground. The pelvis should not sway and there should not be a flexed posture	– is the head kept in midline? – is the child heavy to hold? – are the child's arms kept close to his body? – when the child moves sideways or turns, is it more difficult to move in one direction than the other?

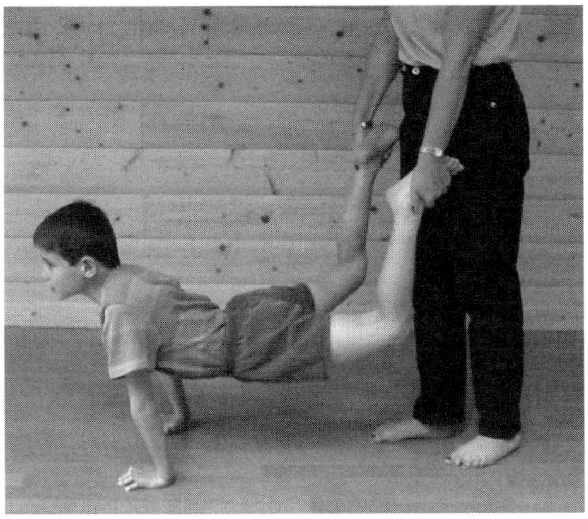

'Wheelbarrows'

Assessment	Considerations
C. Non-weight bearing: Pouring beakers of water/sand/lentils from one to the other	– does the child spill any of the contents? – is one beaker resting on top of the other? – are the beakers kept close to the body? – does the child gain fixation by leaning elbows on his trunk? – is the trunk flexed?

HIP STABILITY

This relates to the joint laxity and the muscle strength of, and around, the hips. It is required for activities such as standing on one leg, hopping and kicking a ball. Together with shoulder and trunk control it has an important role in balance.

Assessment	Considerations
A. Statically: standing on one leg The child should stand on one leg with the raised leg kept away from the weight-bearing leg. The leg on which the child is standing should be extended at the hip and knee and the arms should rest by the child's side. The length of time the child can maintain the position should be documented. The trunk should also be extended	– is the head in midline? – is there overuse of the hip internal rotators? – is the lifted leg adducted and flexed? – are there associated movements?

Standing on one leg correctly

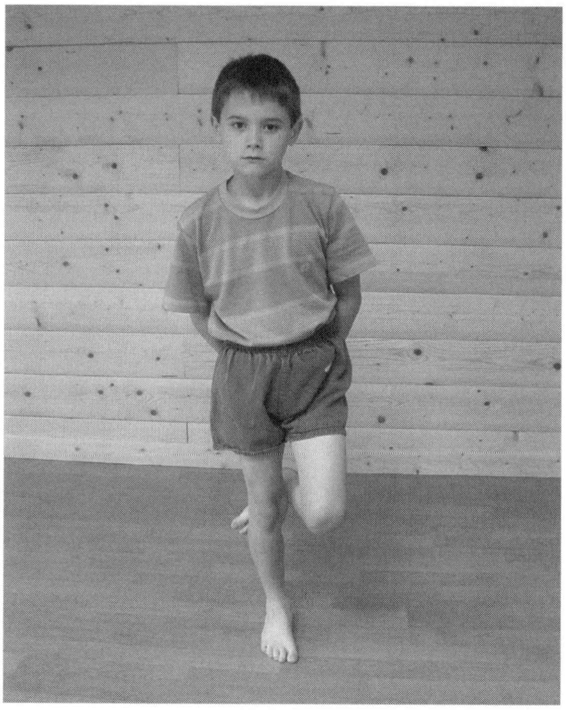

Standing on one leg incorrectly (one leg is hooked around the other)

Assessment	Considerations
A. Statically: high kneeling The child kneels with the hips extended so that the pelvis is away from the heels. There should be equal weight distribution through both sides of the body and the knees should be placed together in a horizontal line. The feet should be resting on the floor and the arms down by the child's side	– is there flexion at the hips? – is there trunk side flexion? – are there any associated movements? – is there protrusion of the stomach and increased lumbar lordosis (i.e. poor anterior tip of the pelvis)?
A. Statically: half kneeling The child should high kneel and place one foot forwards with the hip and knee of that leg flexed to 90 degrees. The foot should rest flat on the	– can the child balance when transferring weight? – is the child able to cross his midline?

floor. The child's arms should rest down by his side. The trunk should be extended and the hip of the side with the knee resting on the floor should also be extended

- how much weight is on the weight-bearing leg?
- is the posture flexed?
- are there associated movements?

Half-kneeling position

B. Dynamically:

1. The child should step stand with one foot on the therapist's lap. The child is asked to reach up with both hands for an object to the non-weight-bearing side and then place the object down by the side of his weight-bearing leg. There should be full extension with rotation of the trunk when reaching for the object and flexion and rotation of the trunk when placing the object on the floor

- is the child able to cross his midline?
- how much weight is on the weight-bearing leg?
- is the posture flexed?

2. Heel to toe walking: the child should be able to walk with one foot in front of the other along a line without losing his balance and with an extended trunk posture

- are there associated movements?

3. Kneel-walking backwards: the child should be able to walk backwards on his knees with equal steps taken, an extended posture and without circumducting the hips when bringing the lifted leg behind him

- are there associated movements?
- does the child lose his balance?

ACTIVE TRUNK EXTENSION

There is often a predominance of flexion patterns which is maintained in activities such as rolling or movement against gravity. It is related to the muscle strength of the back muscles and is required for trunk control.

Assessment	Considerations
Aeroplanes The child is instructed to lie on his stomach on the floor with his arms out in front of him and his legs straight. He is asked to lift his head, arms and legs and maintain the position for as long as possible. The child should be timed to see how long he can hold the position. The arms and legs should remain extended.	– is there asymmetry in weight bearing? – do the knees or arms flex after a certain period of time?

'Aeroplane' position

Assessment	Considerations
Lifting head and shoulders in prone The child is instructed to lie on his stomach on the floor with his arms placed by his side. He is asked to lift his head and shoulders. The length of time the child is able to achieve the task is noted	– is the head in midline? – are the legs straight?

ACTIVE TRUNK FLEXION

This relates to the strength of the stomach muscles and is required for trunk control.

Assessment	Considerations
Curl-ups The child is instructed to lie on his back with his knees flexed and brought up to his chest. The knees are then hugged against the chest by the arms. The head is lifted so the chin is on the chest. The child is instructed to hold the position for as long as possible	– is there asymmetry in weight bearing? – does the child fall to one side in particular?

ROTATION

Assessment	Considerations
Rolling in a straight line The child is asked to lie on the floor and to roll the length of the room. He should be able to initiate the movement from his pelvis followed by his shoulders and head. The child should be able to maintain full extension of his body and be able to roll in a straight line for the whole length. Repeat activity holding a small ball above his head	– is the movement the same to the right and left side? – can rolling be done in an extended posture?

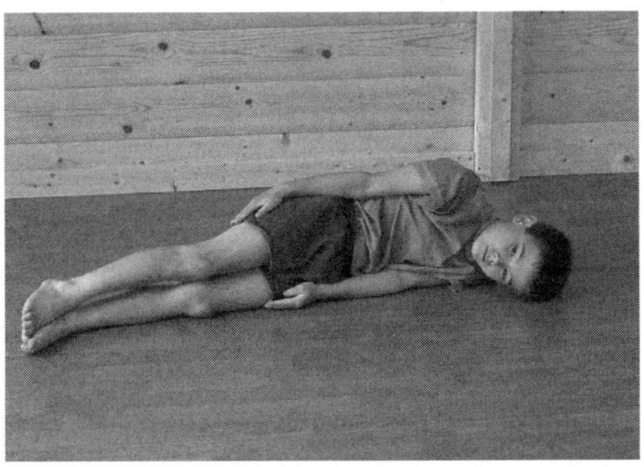

Rolling

Rolling in full extension with arms kept above head

Kneel sitting with arms folded The child is asked to kneel sit with arms folded and to move to one side (so he goes into side sitting) and back again. The child should be able to achieve the task to either side without falling to one side or reaching out with one hand to save himself	– is the posture flexed? – can the child do the activity to one side only?

EYE/HAND CO-ORDINATION

This is the ability of the hands and eyes to work together and is needed for all hand functions such as catching and throwing balls as well as writing. For the following tests, the therapist should document how far from the child they stood. The activity should be repeated a specific number of times – the outcome measures for dyspraxia (Lee 2000) recommend repeating the activity five times.

Assessment	Considerations
Throwing underarm a large ball (football size) and a small ball (tennis size) both with two hands and with alternate hands	– is there enough force for the ball to reach the other person? – is the direction good enough to allow the other person to catch the ball?
Bouncing a ball to another person both with two hands and with alternate hands	– does the child know where to bounce the ball on the floor so that it will reach the other person? – is there enough force and good direction?
Catching a large and small ball with two hands and one hand To start, the hands should be resting by the side. The child should be able to catch the ball by bringing one or both hands out in front of him	– is the child able to track the ball with his eyes? – is catching better on the dominant side? – does the child bring his hands into his body to catch the ball, indicating poor shoulder control?
Throwing the ball into the air and catching to self with both a large and a small ball This is tested both with two hands and with each hand	– is eye tracking good? – is the ball thrown directly above the child or behind or in front of him? – does the child catch the ball away from the body or bring his hand out to catch it? – for a child over seven years of age, can he clap his hands before catching the ball with one hand (Gubbay 1975a)? – does the child stay still when carrying out the task?
Bouncing the ball on the floor and catching to self with both large and small balls This is tested both with two hands and with each hand	– is the child able to bounce the ball directly in front of him with enough force for the ball to reach his hand? – does the child watch the ball? – for a child over seven years of age can he clap his hands before catching the ball with one hand (Gubbay 1975a)? – does the child stay still when carrying out the activity?

EYE/FOOT CO-ORDINATION

This is the ability of the feet and eyes to work together and is required for kicking, walking around obstacles or objects on the floor as well as walking over rough surfaces and stairs. For the following activities, the distance from the child should be documented. The activity should be repeated a specific number of times – the outcome measures for dyspraxia (Lee 2000) recommend repeating the activity five times.

Assessment	Considerations
Kicking balls with either foot to another person The ball should be kicked with enough force and direction to another person in order for that person to be able to stop and trap the ball. The ball should roll along the floor and not be kicked into the air	– consider any difficulties with pelvic control – are there any difficulties with rhythm, timing, directional and spatial awareness?
Stopping a kicked ball with either foot	– is the child able to place his foot on top of the ball? – are there difficulties with pelvic control?

DIRECTIONAL AWARENESS

This is the ability to move in different directions such as forwards, backwards and sideways and should be observed throughout the assessment. Directional awareness is related to the development of the body perception and symmetrical and bilateral integration (for an explanation of these terms see below). The child should be able to move equally in different directions (i.e. forwards, backwards, sideways and diagonally); this ability can be observed when the child is walking, running, jumping and hopping.

Assessment	Considerations
Ask the child to walk forwards, backwards, sideways and diagonally across a room	– does the child turn to the direction to which he is travelling?
Writing in a straight line	– consider difficulties with shoulder control, eye/hand co-ordination, spatial awareness and midline crossing
Writing letters and achieving cursive writing	– is the writing smooth and is there good transition of left/right and up/down which is needed for automatic joined-up writing?

MIDLINE CROSSING

This is the ability to cross one side of the body to the other side across the imaginary midline in the centre of the body (i.e. either an arm or leg from one side of the body to the other) and is associated with the development of efficient two-handed ability. It is necessary for activities such as writing. When difficulties are apparent, it is indicative of deficits in dominance/laterality and bilateral integration. A great deal of work has been carried out by Mitchell and Wood (1999) who used the last three tests in Table 3.8 for assessing midline crossing as a screening tool for three-year-olds.

Assessment	Considerations
Throwing and catching balls across self The child should throw and catch the ball with two hands diagonally across himself to the therapist	– consider shoulder control, eye/hand co-ordination and directional awareness
Passing bean bags from one side to the other	– does the differing eye/hand dominance affect the ability to one side? – does the child have a tendency to throw the bean bag rather than place it? – does the child turn into the direction of movement?
Ask the child to cross one foot over the other	– does the child understand the instruction 'to cross'? – the foot should cross completely over the other one
Ask the child to cross one knee over the other	– the knee should completely cross over the other one
Cross arms and place hands on knees, shoulders and ears	– does the child know where his knees, shoulders and ears are? – can the child cross his arms completely? – do the hands land on the specific points?

Taking bean bags from one side to the other in long sitting

SPATIAL AWARENESS

This is the ability of the child to judge distances and direction of his position in relation to other objects. It should be checked specifically if the child is complaining of knocking over drinks or bumping into things. Spatial awareness is related to body perception and directional sense. This should be observed throughout the assessment. The therapist should be aware of whether the child sits appropriately on a chair without missing it. In addition, the child should be able to move around a room without knocking into furniture. When negotiating an obstacle course he should be able to go under and through obstacles without bumping into them. The child should also be able to place himself in accordance with instructions, e.g. 'Stand with your feet behind the line.'

Assessment	Considerations
Observe the child writing on a plain piece of paper He should be able to use the whole paper and not just one section of it	– are there difficulties with shoulder control, eye/hand co-ordination and directional awareness?
Ask the child to run the length of a room which has five cones or skittles placed 45cm apart in the middle of the room The child should be able to run in and out of the skittles without knocking them over and in the fastest possible speed	– consider any difficulties with eye/foot co-ordination as well as pelvic stability and directional awareness

SYMMETRICAL INTEGRATION

This is the ability to move both sides of the body simultaneously in identical patterns of movements. It should be assessed if the child is having problems such as fastening buttons. The activity should be repeated a specific number of times – the outcome measures for dyspraxia (Lee 2000) recommend repeating the activity ten times.

Assessment	Considerations
Jumping forwards and backwards The child should be able to initiate the movement and land with both feet together	– is the general posture flexed or extended? – are there any associated movements?
Throwing a ball with both hands The ball should be thrown with equal force from both hands	– is there poor eye/hand co-ordination?
Throwing two small balls (one in each hand) into a box at the same time	– keep the movement continuous to see if there is a break-up of continuation – are there any associated movements?

BILATERAL INTEGRATION

Bilateral integration is the ability to move both sides of the body simultaneously in opposing patterns of movement such as jumping sideways. It is particularly important to assess if the child has difficulty using a knife and fork. For children who show difficulty in this area, consideration should be given to where they sit in the classroom, especially if the child sits on a table with others to the side of the teacher or to the board.

Assessment	Considerations
Jumping to the side The child should initiate the movement and land with both feet together	– does the child turn to the side to which he is travelling? – consider directional awareness – is the posture flexed or extended?
The child sits at a table and taps the foot and finger on the same side together and then repeats the task on the opposite side The child should complete 30 alternate taps in 30 seconds (Lee and Smith 1998).	

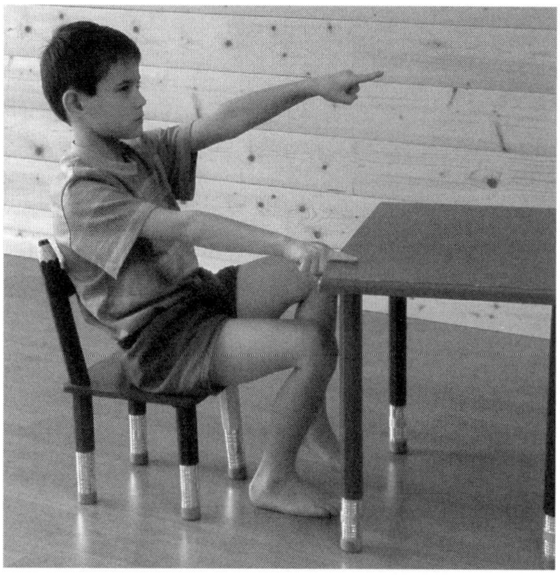

Alternate tapping with finger and foot

KNOWLEDGE OF THE TWO SIDES

This is the early development of laterality which culminates in a child's thorough understanding of the left and right side and the dominance of one side. Children with dyspraxia are often unable to recognise that the two sides are different.

Assessment	Considerations
Ask the child to perform an activity with one arm/hand and to repeat the activity on the opposite side	– does the child repeat the activity on the same side?

DOMINANCE OF ONE SIDE

Children may not have a preferred dominance but it is necessary for hand function activities such as writing. Problems in this area can lead to poor interaction of the two sides and directional confusion.

Assessment	Considerations
Ask the child to choose a ball when it is offered to him in midline	– does the child use either hand? – does the child throw one-handed, with both hands or does he swap hands? – if the child is having difficulty with writing it may not be due to poor dominance of one side but due to poor shoulder stability, eye/hand co-ordination, bilateral integration, directional or spatial awareness or midline crossing
Threading activity	– does the child swap the hand of major manipulation with the assisting hand?
Ask the child to kick a ball which is placed between the feet	– does the child have a preference to kick with one foot? – if asked to kick a ball several times he should use his preferred foot all the time; difficulty with kicking balls may also be due to problems with pelvic stability, eye/foot co-ordination, posture, directional and spatial awareness
Climbing onto a box/step up onto the stairs	– which foot moves onto the first step?
With the child standing, gently push him forwards	– which foot moves forward first?
Ask the child to look through a hole on a piece of paper (which is raised to his face for him with the hole in the midline position) or through a keyhole	– which eye does the child use and, if asked to do the activity frequently, does he always choose the same eye?

RHYTHM AND TIMING

This should be taken into account in all activities. Some tasks should be fast and some slow.

Assessment	Considerations
'Pat a Cake' Clapping hands in time with the therapist	– if the child is having difficulty with this task consider whether it may be due to shoulder control and eye/hand co-ordination as opposed to rhythm and timing
Using a drum, ask the child to listen first and then copy the rhythm	– consider any difficulties with shoulder control and eye/hand co-ordination

BODY PERCEPTION AND PROPRIOCEPTION

This includes body image (the visual knowledge of oneself), body scheme (the sensory knowledge of oneself), and body awareness (the sensory knowledge of oneself moving through space). It is particularly important to assess this area for the movement-seeking child, i.e. one who cannot sit still in the classroom or at the dinner table.

Assessment	Considerations
Walking up and down stairs with eyes closed or backwards The child should be able to achieve the task reciprocally and without tripping	– consider (if there is difficulty) that it may be due to spatial awareness and to kinaesthesia difficulties

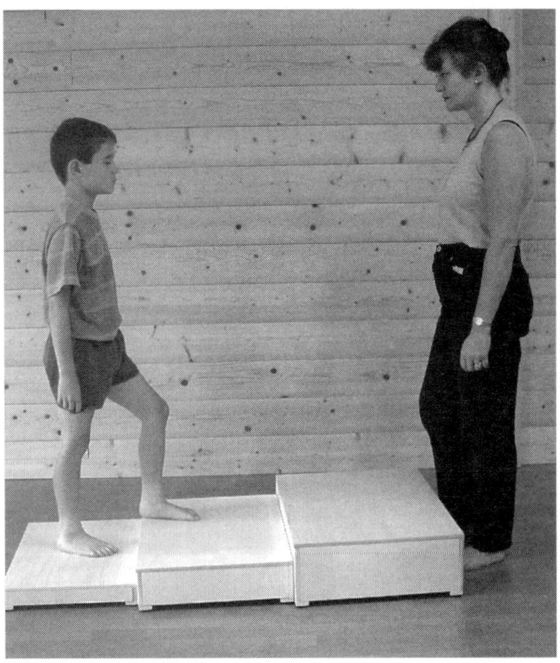

Walking up steps with eyes closed

Assessment	Considerations
Face to face, copying the therapist's movements	– are there problems with the knowledge of two sides?
Dressing The child should be able to take off, and put on, his clothes unaided. It should be noted that dressing involves many skills which include crossing midline, knowledge of the concept of back and front and inside out plus co-ordination	
Holding objects Consider the amount of pressure used to hold objects	– does the child spill liquids, break pencil leads, throw a ball too hard/too gently?

VISUAL AND AUDITORY INTERPRETATION

Visual interpretation is the ability to copy movements previously shown to the child and in the assessment will have been noted during activities. It is expected that all children should be able to copy at least three activities. Older children (i.e. from eight years) should be able to complete at least four activities. Ensure that the tasks given are those that the child can complete. Auditory interpretation is the ability to carry out spoken commands. The child should be given at least three or four activities to complete.

Example for visual short-term memory

The child is asked to watch the therapist while she carries out a sequence of three or more activities such as walking around in a circle, jumping in the air with both feet together and taking a step forward. The child is then asked to carry out the sequences in the correct order.

Example for verbal short-term memory

The child is instructed to listen to commands and to carry them out in the correct order, e.g. a clap, a step, a hop and jump.

GROSS MOTOR SEQUENCING

This is the ability to carry out a specified number of activities (which may involve number and direction) in the correct order.

Assessment	Considerations
Ask the child to carry out 2–4 tasks together, e.g. jumping, hopping, clapping Include number and direction with the tasks	– are there problems with auditory interpretation or recall? – are there problems with directional awareness?

KINAESTHESIA

This is the ability of the brain to know the position and movement of parts of the body.

Assessment	Considerations
Walking up and down stairs with eyes looking forward The child should be able to reciprocally walk up and down stairs without feeling for the next step with his foot	– consider body perception and proprioception

Walking up steps looking directly in front

Example for the assessment of kinaesthesia

The therapist places one of the child's arms in abduction and lateral rotation at the shoulder and 90 degrees flexion at the elbow. The child is asked to place his other arm in the identical position (other arm positions can be used).

MOTOR PLANNING

The ability to plan the necessary movements that are required to move from one position to another may be difficult for a child if he is showing problems with task organisation or essay construction.

Assessment	Considerations
Building Lego and other constructional activities The child can be asked: to make his own construction; what he is making; to make something specific such as a car, house, etc.	
Making up own obstacle course	– if the child has difficulty with this activity, consider that there may be difficulties with spatial and directional awareness, rhythm, timing and posture – does the child show fear of carrying out the activities of an obstacle course or is he unaware of his own limitations?
Climbing over 2–4 chairs and then crawl through under the chairs 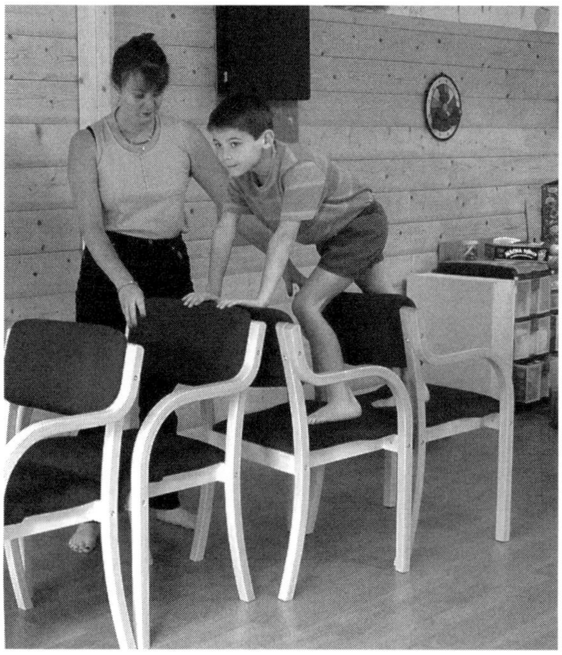 *Climbing over chairs*	– is the child able to climb onto the first chair, stand up, and climb over the back onto the next chair? – is there any anxiety? – can the child climb down from the last chair forwards easily? – can the child crawl under the chairs easily? – consider difficulties with balance, spatial and directional awareness

SELF-ORGANISATIONAL SKILLS

This is the ability to work out the correct sequences for activities of daily living.

Assessment	Considerations
Making a sandwich – verbally described and then demonstrated The child should be able to explain and show the following:	
• Two pieces of bread are required • Butter spread onto them • A filling applied • The second piece of bread placed on top • Sandwich placed on the plate and/or cut in half • The sandwich is then eaten	– does the child know what his favourite sandwich is? – is the child hesitant or does he backtrack with sequences? – does the child use any utensils such as a knife?

Making a sandwich

Assessment	Considerations
Brushing teeth The child should demonstrate and explain the following:	
• Place toothpaste on the brush • Put it in the mouth • Move it up and down and side to side • Rinse mouth • Put toothpaste and brush away	– are there difficulties with co-ordination skills? – does the child backtrack with sequences?

Stamina

Generally, children with dyspraxia have poor stamina and tire quickly. This is an important consideration when carrying out the assessment as the child may not be able to complete all the active tasks in one session (e.g. hopping, running and jumping). Carrying out an objective fitness test (such as the Multistage Fitness Test) may be useful to reveal the actual fitness of the child and to monitor the improvement at the end of treatment objectively.

Fine motor skills: assessment

The assessment of fine motor skill can be carried out by the use of standardised tests (the merits of which have already been discussed on p. 20) and by informal observational assessment – it is important to use a combination approach. When performing a fine motor task, the head, eyes, hand and trunk function as a unit, therefore consideration must be given to all aspects that may interfere with the process and adversely affect the outcome (see pp. 85–92 for a list of skills required).

Some of the available standardised assessments include (see also Appendix 1):

- Bruininks-Oseretsky Test of Motor Proficiency
- Movement Assessment Battery for Children
- Peabody Developmental Motor Scales (early years assessment, birth to five years)

Poor fine motor skills affect the child's ability in all areas of his life:

- Self-help: fastenings when dressing, buttons, zips and laces, cutlery use, opening crisp packets, cartons, etc.
- Play – a child's play is his work: toys with small parts.
- School: interferes with writing, use of scissors, design technology.

Importantly, the assessment needs to consider the issue of self-esteem. The child may struggle with so many aspects of his life that the situation becomes self-limiting, i.e. the child avoids doing the very things he needs to do in order to improve functional ability. It is not uncommon to find that children with adequate or good gross motor co-ordination experience specific difficulty with many areas of fine motor skills, especially handwriting.

Handwriting: assessment

A problem with handwriting performance is one of the most common fine-motor skill difficulties, resulting in referral of school-age children to an occupational therapist (Oliver 1990; Cermak 1991). Handwriting is the 'graphic' result of motor, perceptual and cognitive processes and is one of the most complex skills we learn (and teach). Most children have a variety of pre-school writing experiences but they can vary considerably. In this above all other activities, avoidance can become an early established pattern: 'John has never been interested in painting or colouring!'

The demands of class sizes and variation in teacher experience often mean that the results of the graphic process are seen and not the 'mechanics' of the construction. This may give rise to the formation of persistently bad habits. There are many commercially available handwriting evaluations, mostly based on measuring the child's functional performance of writing, but few provide enough guidelines on how to assess underlying deficits. Many of these are 'normed' in the US and as a result are not always applicable. Standardised tests which can be used as predictors of likely problems to support informal assessment include:

- **Beery-Butenica –Visual Motor Integration** as a measure of visual-motor skill was found to be significant in predicting the accuracy of handwriting performance (see Appendix 1). The child is deemed ready for formal instruction only if able to copy accurately a vertical and horizontal line, circle, cross, right oblique line, square, left oblique line and oblique cross.
- **Test of Visual Perceptual Skills – Revised (TVPS-R) Gardner** is a test that focuses on perceptual skills rather than motor skills and may predict likely difficulties with spatial elements, e.g. problems with letter size, slant, etc. (see Appendix 1).
- **Motor-Free Visual Perceptual Test – Revised (MVPT-R)** is a simpler version of the previous test, suitable for younger children with a shorter administration time.

A detailed assessment should include the following:

- Availability of differing samples of work, e.g. copied or creative.
- History of performance from pre-writing onwards including teacher/parent opinions, child's confidence or otherwise, any relevant health/medical issues.
- Direct observations of the child at work.
- Examination of the following:
  - posture, position (furniture/child), shoulder stability, etc.
  - quality of the mechanics, i.e. letter formation, slant, spacing, size, etc.
- Use of supporting assessments – visual-motor integration, non-motor visual perception, functional ocular motor performance.

Problems of assessing younger children

A young child may not be as co-operative as an older child in which case an observational assessment is required. The child should be provided with an age-appropriate environment in which he is able to explore a variety of different challenges, e.g. climbing, jumping, crawling, conceptual opportunities, under, down, over in a series of game-like situations. A clear understanding is needed of the age-appropriate abilities such as ball skills, motor planning, short-term memory and hand function. The key to improving a child's performance lies in early accurate assessment and treatment. It is important to note that competence changes with age.

Interpretation of the assessment

This can now be used to plan intervention. Accurate interpretation involves interpreting clusters of symptoms to form a profile of the child's difficulties. Accurate interpretation of what we see is essential and good interpretation only comes from experience.

- Do not be too quick to provide a diagnostic label.
- Assessment may take several sessions.
- Ensure that physiotherapy or occupational therapy will be able to assist the difficulties.
- Wait until you have all the results and interpret them in a holistic way.
- Consider differential diagnosis.
- Use clinical observations to improve the accuracy of your assessment.
- Use the findings of assessment to identify the correct treatment method for each individual child.

Recording the assessment

It is important that the assessment is clearly written, concise and can be understood by other professionals as well as by the parents and child. The following guidelines on what to include in the assessment may be helpful:

History
- reason for the referral;
- birth history;
- medical history;
- relevant previous assessments and treatments;
- age of reaching milestones;
- difficulties that the child is currently experiencing;
- concerns from the parents and school.

General impression
- how the child presented, e.g. happy, talkative, quiet;
- concentration skills;
- self-confidence and self-esteem;
- child's likes and dislikes at school;
- child's hobbies.

General assessment
- this should be the main bulk of the assessment documentation and should be related directly to the results of the assessment and the test scores.

Summary of the main problems/difficulties found

Recommendations
- what treatment is required;
- how many treatment sessions are required;
- what the home programme will involve;
- when reviews will take place;
- when treatment will take place;
- explanations given to the parents and child.

Objectives as set by the therapist with review dates (see below)

Goals set by the parents and child (see below)

Objectives

The objectives are short term. They will be specific tasks that will be used to monitor the child's progress and the outcome of the intervention. They need to be realistic – a separate objective is required for each area of difficulty found. Each objective should be reviewed at the time of the child's review assessment.

Examples of objectives

- Improve shoulder control so that the child is able to carry out 60 steps of wheelbarrows without the pelvis swaying side to side and with the hands pointing directly in front of him.
- Improve pelvic control so that the child is able to stand on one leg for 15+ seconds, able to walk backwards on his knees with no circumduction of the hips and able to stand on one leg.
- Improve eye/hand co-ordinations so that the child is able to catch a tennis ball five out of five times with one hand and throw with good direction.

- Improve eye/foot co-ordination so that the child is able to trap a ball with either foot/kick a ball with good direction.
- Improve short-term memory so that the child is able to carry out three sequences (when shown and asked of him) in the correct order.

Goals

These are generally set in consultation with the parents and child and are related to those activities (at home and school) they wish to be improved. The goals must be identified at the start of therapy. The child must understand and make clear his own priorities, e.g. better handwriting, wants to ride his bike, etc. It must be stressed that in order for the assessment and treatment to be successful a functional outcome is paramount.

Examples of goals

- The child does not fall or trip over.
- The child is able to participate more readily in PE and games.
- The child finds it easier to carry out ball activities.
- To improve messy eating.
- The child is able to carry objects without dropping them.
- Improvement in self-confidence.
- To be able to write more quickly and for the writing to be legible.

It is important to give teachers clear and relevant support – Chapter 4 discusses how support and advice may be given to the school. If the child's problems involve learning, goals must be directed towards an improvement in the classroom that can be monitored by the therapist or teacher. The educational implications for intervention *must* be emphasised in the report which may be part of a statement of special needs (see Association of Paediatric Chartered Physiotherapists 1997).

Linking assessment and management is an excellent way to ensure that positive help is provided after the assessment. Time spent on using a team approach to planning the intervention will be time well spent; several different approaches may be indicated after assessment using skills from different disciplines.

Chapter 4

Treatment

At what age can treatment start?

Opinions differ on the age at which to start intervention. In my experience, however, the earlier the treatment begins the better to help ensure that the child does not lose self-confidence and self-esteem. It will assist with alleviating many behavioural problems as well as helping the child to succeed physically, emotionally, socially and academically. A child begins to compare himself with his peers by the age of six to seven years, therefore it is important to ensure that treatment begins before this time. But it is never too late to commence treatment – Lee and Smith (1998) concluded from their study of children aged 4–14 that children in secondary school made just as much improvement as those in junior school.

It is important to consider the child's age when deciding on the appropriate type of treatment. Certainly a young child (i.e. under the age of three) may have difficulty with a very structured and formal treatment (ideas are discussed later in the chapter). Treatment continues where the assessment left off. It is important that the child finds the treatment fun and enjoyable; he must feel he is succeeding.

Treatment methods

There is a range of different options for intervention available to the therapist, some of which are included below.

Skill acquisition

Specific areas of dysfunction are identified on assessment and as a result specific therapy programmes are developed to improve these individual skills. For example, a child who has been found to have difficulty with gross motor skills (specifically kicking a ball and hopping on one leg) may benefit from this form of intervention. The child's difficulties may be caused by lack of experience or slow maturation (see 'Treatment' section below for a more detailed description of treatment).

Sensory integration

This form of therapy has been developed from the work initially pioneered by Dr A. Jean Ayres. Treatment is child-oriented and aims to provide a sensory environment in which children can actively explore new skills. Therapy will help to co-ordinate the two sides of the body, improve organisation and develop self-image and confidence. Techniques include vestibular, proprioceptive and tactile inputs.

Perceptuo-motor

Frostig and Kephart (popular from the mid-1950s) are examples of this method that involves a sequence of training tasks which the child repeats until he becomes competent at performing them. Progression to a harder or more complex task then follows. An educational programme based on visual perceptual skills, the tasks include spatial, eye/hand co-ordination, form consistency and figure/ground discrimination tasks (Frostig and Horne 1964).

Neuro-developmental

This method describes a form of intervention particularly related to the management of cerebral palsy (Bobath and Bobath 1975). By inhibiting increase tone through handling and positioning, more normal patterns of movement are facilitated. Gordon and McKinlay (1980) describe 'clumsiness' as a neuro-developmental problem resulting from immature brain development. The cerebellum is particularly vulnerable to processes affecting brain growth in late pregnancy and early infancy, and damage may result (evidenced by immaturity of motor development).

Psycho-motor therapy (Naville)

This form of treatment was brought to the UK by occupational therapist Lorraine Burr. She worked closely with physiotherapist Judi Baker in the use of relevant aspects of this treatment for physiotherapy and occupational therapy. It is considered that poor co-ordination is due to physical, social and psychological problems. Gross motor skills, exercises, dissociation, co-ordination and relaxation are used for treatment and body image, laterality and awareness of time and space; and auditory and visual memory are trained (Baker 1981).

Kinaesthetic sensitivity

Kinaesthetic sensitivity has been described as the ability of the brain to know the position and movement of parts of the body. Laszlo and Bairstow (1990), who have researched extensively in this area, consider kinaesthesia to be one of the factors in the control of motor behaviour. They have developed specific remedial kits where vision is withdrawn. One test involves discriminating height on two inclined runways and the other test involves the child tracing around a stencilled pattern. Children practise on a daily basis for two weeks in order to improve their kinaesthetic awareness. The tests are used in conjunction with a general motor programme to improve the child's motor skills.

The Lee method

The main objectives of treatment are to improve proximal stability to allow for a point of fixation, improve self-confidence, self-esteem, co-ordination (both eye/foot and eye/hand), memory, planning and organisational skills. Specific exercises are carried out to increase muscle strength and games and activities are played to improve skills. The emphasis of treatment is on making it fun, ensuring that skills are broken down to a level at which the child can achieve before building upon them. The aim is to help each child to reach age-appropriate levels with all their skills. A long-term management programme is devised for each child following treatment which is updated yearly. Treatment consists of a weekly session for eight weeks which is supplemented by two home programmes each lasting four weeks to ensure that the child does not become bored with the exercises and activities.

The most popular forms of therapy

The most popular forms of intervention are skill acquisition, neuro-developmental, sensory integration, perceptuo-motor and the Lee method. These forms of intervention all have differing theoretical bases and the therapist must understand the basic philosophies and have received appropriate training before using the principles of each form of intervention. As each child is different and will respond differently to intervention, it is important that the therapist is able to tailor different forms of treatment to suit a particular child.

Assessment does not necessarily mean that a child will receive therapy but their needs for intervention are identified. Children whose problems are affecting their everyday function, who are depressed, anxious, withdrawn or under stress, obviously need help. This may be provided by a psychologist, physiotherapist, occupational therapist, speech and language therapist, parent, teacher or classroom assistant. The therapist can instruct the classroom helper, teacher or parent to carry out an intervention programme but the initial assessment and regular review should, wherever possible, be provided by a therapist.

It is vital to be able to determine those groups of children that will do well in therapy, those children who, with training tasks, will improve their skill levels, those for whom sensory integrative therapy is most appropriate and those children for whom therapy is *not* the right answer. Some children may benefit from a more global approach rather than a specific treatment programme. Close working practice with the therapist in school is necessary.

Therapy should only be started if the therapist is able to monitor the progress of the child. If within four weeks there is no change in the child, the team should review whether their diagnosis, assessment and its interpretation were accurate and what modifications are needed to their approach.

Record-keeping and monitoring are addressed under a different heading (p. 77), but evaluation and monitoring are essential to the success of the intervention. Time should always be allocated for this purpose.

Treatment

The treatment session

As with the assessment, the same considerations apply to both the room and the therapist. The child should wear the correct clothing such as PE kit or shorts and a T-shirt. Some children may find that an hour's session is too long to maintain concentration and will need to take a short break halfway through.

Individual versus group treatment

Group therapy

Group intervention is always fun provided there is adequate adult supervision and support. It should be noted that group therapy is not a means for assisting with lack of resources since these children require a high staff supervision ratio. Some children treated in groups may need initial therapy on an individual basis until sufficient confidence is gained to succeed in a small group situation. When organising groups, careful consideration should be given to ensure that children with similar interests and abilities are placed together in order to gain maximum benefit. In addition, the activities should be carefully planned to ensure that the children's interest is maintained continuously. It is important that children are given home programmes so that newly acquired skills may be practised to ensure that they are perfected.

Group activities help the child to be aware of others, aid learning by watching and using others in partnership (Sherbourne 1990; Russell 1988; Fink 1989), and teach children about sharing and taking turns. Friends and siblings can be offered places within the clubs provided that sufficient thought is given to how the activities are organised (i.e. not all competitive).

Individual therapy

Treating children on an individual basis allows for close supervision so that those with poor concentration can be closely monitored throughout the session. Individual therapy also allows more decision-making by the child. Again, treatment sessions need to be well planned in advance to ensure that the child does not lose concentration and that all areas of difficulties are covered in the treatment sessions.

Table 4.1 Advantages and disadvantages of group therapy

Advantages	*Disadvantages*
• Allows for competition	• Requires a lot of supervision
• Allows the child to meet other children like himself	• Needs to be well planned
• Allows the child to learn social skills	• Only children with similar difficulties may be treated together
• Allows the parents to meet together	• Does not always allow the therapist the opportunity to discuss the child's individual difficulties with parents on a one-to-one basis or give time for parent/child relationship
	• Large space required

Table 4.2 Advantages and disadvantages of individual treatment

Advantages	*Disadvantages*
• Assists with poor concentration	• Minimal competition (only with therapist and parent)
• Assists with poor self-esteem	• Minimal assistance with social skills
• Allows the child to make decisions	• Does not allow the child to meet other children with similar difficulties
• Small space is required	• Does not allow the parents opportunity to meet other parents
• Gives time for parent/child relationship	

Planning a treatment session

The treatment sessions

Most treatment sessions are one hour in duration. Approximately 20 minutes is spent on muscle-strengthening exercises, i.e. carrying out the exercises from the home programme. This verifies that the child is completing the exercises correctly and can cope with increasing the number of repetitions per week. Generally, three exercises for shoulder control and pelvic control are practised and one or two exercises for back extension if these areas initially were shown to be weak. It is important to change the exercises regularly as children often become easily bored. Exercises usually are carried out starting with ten repetitions and increased by five repetitions weekly until the child is completing a maximum of 40 (30 repetitions for the younger child, i.e. under six). As the child's strength improves, the number of exercises is reduced to ensure that the child is not spending too long on the programme at home.

Five to ten minutes is then allocated to stamina work such as using the trampoline or circuit work. This is followed by five to ten minutes of co-ordination skills. The remainder of the time is spent using games and activities to assist with other areas of difficulties. Treatment sessions should be planned in advance so that the therapist knows which areas s/he will be working on in the session and which activities and games need to be prepared. An example of how sessions may be planned ensuring that all areas of difficulties are treated is given below.

Session planning

Session 1

30 minutes	5 minutes	25 minutes
teach home programme inc. ball skills	stamina	games, e.g. eye/hand, memory

Session 2

20 minutes	5 minutes	5 minutes	20–30 minutes
check home programme	co-ordination	stamina	midline crossing, eye/foot and eye/hand co-ordination

Session 3

20 minutes	5 minutes	5 minutes	20–30 minutes
check home programme	co-ordination	stamina	spatial awareness, memory, symmetrical and bilateral integration

Session 4

20 minutes	5 minutes	5 minutes	20–30 minutes
check home programme	co-ordination	stamina	eye/hand and eye/foot co-ordination, midline crossing

Session 5

30 minutes	5 minutes	5 minutes	20 minutes
teach second home programme	co-ordination	stamina	planning and self-organisational skills, symmetrical and bilateral integration

Session 6

20 minutes	5 minutes	5 minutes	20–30 minutes
check home programme	co-ordination	stamina	planning, co-ordination, self-organisational skills, memory

Session 7

15 minutes	5 minutes	5 minutes	35 minutes
check home programme	co-ordination	stamina	midline crossing, self-organisational skills, planning and memory

Session 8

45–50 minutes	10 minutes
checklist to ascertain progress to date – retest all areas of difficulty initially seen and compare scores	discuss with parents and child plan until review

Table 4.3 Planning a treatment session

Considerations	*Discussion*
How will the child relate to you – as a teacher or a friend? How will he address you?	A combination of both teacher and friend works well. Being called Mrs/Miss/Mr will give authority and may work well for the older child but not always for younger children
How will you ensure that the child is happy to come back and be eager to participate in treatment?	Make the treatment as fun as possible and do not set activities that are too hard to complete
How do you build up the child's concentration and reduce his distractibility?	This will occur as the child improves his proximal stability so that he finds it easier to stay in one position. Also, choose games initially that are quick to complete (such as Wiggly Worms or Magnetic Fish) and then progress to games which take longer to complete (such as Magna Force and memory games such as Button Maze and Match Me)
What happens when the novelty has worn off?	Change the exercises regularly and ensure you do different activities each week as well as play different games each session. Lending games for the child to take home may also be beneficial
Some children will not do their programme with a parent or make such a fuss that the parent is unable to do the programme with them. What do you do?	Giving rewards for completing the programme without a fuss (such as stickers) may work. Some children may prefer to do the programme with another member of the family. It is important that the child and parent are made aware of the importance of the home programme if the child is to reach his maximum potential
What do you do if the child and parent report that they feel overloaded with too much work to do at home?	Discuss with the school and parent the amount of homework and additional work the child may be given by other professionals to find a compromise while the therapy is being carried out. Ensure that the child spends no longer than 20 minutes completing the home programme
The school will not allow the child to be treated during school hours	This is difficult since the child will be too tired in the afternoon for treatment and will not generally achieve so much. Discuss the options with the teachers for a compromise such as seeing the child first thing in the morning or during lunch time. Sessions may be staggered so that the child does not miss the same lesson each week
These children do not like change and welcome a regular routine	Ensure wherever possible that the same therapist treats the child at each session. Keep the sessions to a similar format each time

Length of treatments

Blocks of treatment sessions work very well. Many parents and children have reported that they particularly like blocks because:

- there is a set length of time in which to focus on the programme;
- they know it will end and that they will not have to repeat the same things!

Different lengths of blocks have been tried – Lee (2000) reported that eight-week blocks worked well. If treatment time was shorter the children were unable to reach all their goals – if treatment took longer, the children's skills and improvement often reached a plateau and the children became bored.

Some children may require more than one block of treatment and parents should be made aware of this. If this is the case, then the child should be given a break between blocks.

Home programmes

Home programmes are crucial: they allow the treatment to be continued on a regular basis and ensure that muscle strength is improved and skills are practised. By carrying out the programmes regularly, children will gain the maximum benefit from treatment and be able to reach their maximum potential. It is important, however, not to overburden the children and their families with too many activities. The therapist should ensure that the family find an appropriate time in the day in which to complete the programme. Consideration must be given to siblings, homework and quality rest and relaxation time in the evening. The exercises must be easy to do within the home and the programme, which must first be explained carefully by the therapist, should be accompanied by clear instructions on how to do the exercises correctly – pictures can often help the parents to understand the exercise. The amount of time spent on the programme should be carefully considered, taking into account the fact that most children will have homework and extra activities during the week – 15–20 minutes per day is generally considered to be more than adequate.

The programme should be varied to avoid children becoming bored. Few home programmes have considered in detail the format for carrying out treatment at home. The Lee method, however, uses two separate programmes within the eight-week block of treatment. The first programme concentrates on improving the proximal stability as well as co-ordination skills, short-term memory and stamina. The second programme continues with these skills but not as intensively. The emphasis is placed on planning and organisational skills as well as other areas of difficulty. In order to improve muscle strength, the number of repetitions of each exercise must be increased each week. I usually recommend that ten repetitions are used initially increasing by five repetitions per week until the child reaches 40 (children under six can usually only tolerate 30 repetitions maximum).

Treatment ideas

The treatment ideas suggested below represent only some of the activities that can be used for different problem areas. Parents, children and therapists often find that they adapt or make up new games. Therapy *must* always be fun – if a child is enjoying himself he will try his best, feel motivated and learn. Often giving the exercises child-friendly names helps the child to relate to them more easily.

Shoulder stability

- Kneel over a roll (to support the trunk) ensuring that the body weight is kept forward and practise reaching for objects in front and above with alternate hands.
- 'Fruit picking' (Fig. 4.1). Sitting on the side with weight borne by the propped arm, reach up and over with the opposite arm to reach an object and then place it in a box beside the weight-bearing hand.

Figure 4.1

- With the hands on a bench, jump over from side to side of the bench.
- 'Bunny hops' (Fig. 4.2). Jumping with feet side to side and hands resting on a small stool.

Figure 4.2

- 'Bear walking' (Fig. 4.3). Walking on hands and feet with knees off the floor.

Figure 4.3

- Batting a balloon and other batting games.
- Carrying tennis balls on a tennis racket around a room or in and out of obstacles.
- Lying prone over a scooter board, practise propelling it with the arms. Ensure that the whole hand is on the floor and the shoulders are over the board.
- 'Dog's dinner' (Fig. 4.4). On all fours, encourage the child to bring his face towards to the floor and then lift up again as if doing a half press-up.

Figure 4.4

- Crab football.
- 'Crab walking' (Fig. 4.5).

Figure 4.5

- Drawing shapes in the air.
- Writing on a chalk- or white-board.
- Pegging the washing on the washing line.
- 'Policeman directing the traffic'. Arms out to the side with hands level with the shoulders, the child has to direct a person (who is pretending to be a car) around the room by using his arms to show forwards, turning and stop.
- 'Bird flapping wings' (Fig. 4.6). With the arms kept out to the side and the hands level with the shoulders, the child has to gently move his hands up and down while keeping his arms still. This may be progressed with the child holding bean bags or small bats.

Figure 4.6

- Magnetic fishing games (ensure that the elbow is not tucked into the body to give stability to the movement).
- Bouncing therapy balls (using two hands) to another person.
- Throwing medicine balls (2kg or 3kg weights) to another person and catching.
- Whizz ball (Fig. 4.7). The child holds onto the handles of the game and opens his arms out to the side to send the ball along the line to the other person.

Figure 4.7

- Spooning rice from one container to another (Fig. 4.8). This will also assist with eye/hand co-ordination and midline crossing.

Figure 4.8

- Using a rowing machine is especially useful for an older child (Fig. 4.9).

Figure 4.9

Hip stability

- 'Bridging' (Fig. 4.10). Lying on the floor with both knees flexed or with one leg straight (the straight leg should be as close to the floor as possible), ask the child to lift the pelvis and slowly lower it again. For the younger child, a car can be pushed 'under the bridge' when the pelvis is raised.

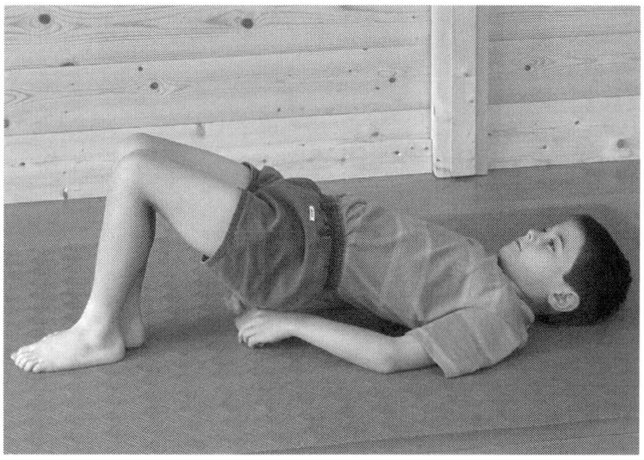

Figure 4.10

- Kneel walking – forwards and backwards and to each side. Ensure the child takes small steps when walking backwards with no circumduction of the hips.
- 'Fruit box' (Fig. 4.11). In high kneeling or half-kneeling position, practise throwing and catching balls or throwing bean bags into different-sized boxes.

Figure 4.11

- 'Scissors' (Fig. 4.12). Lying on his side with the underneath leg bent at the knee and the upper leg extended, ask the child to lift the top leg slowly into the air and then slowly lower it again.

Figure 4.12

- Long sitting – using a tied theraband, abduct (take out) the legs.
- In the crab position, practise walking forwards, backwards or kicking a ball – ensure the pelvis is well lifted.
- 'Squeaky dips' (Fig. 4.13). Standing on a step, practise gently touching the floor with the toes of one foot and then bringing the foot back onto the step. To ensure that the child does not place too much weight through his toes, he can practise this exercise by touching a squeaky toy on the floor without allowing the toy to squeak.

Figure 4.13

- 'Shoe shop' (Fig. 4.14). The child should sit on a chair so that he can place his feet on the floor. One foot is raised and held by the therapist who is sitting on the floor in front of the child. The therapist must also hold the child's hands with her other hand. The child is then asked to stand up slowly and sit down again.

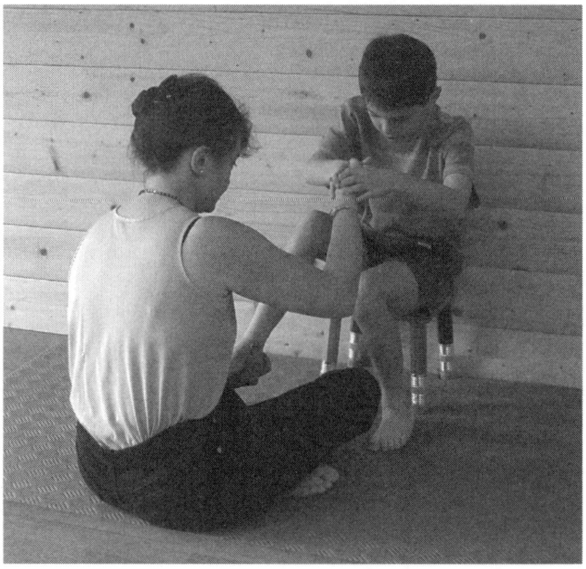

Figure 4.14

- 'Step-ups' (Fig. 4.15). Facing a step, the child is asked to step up leading with one leg and then step down again leading with the same leg.

Figure 4.15

- Pelvic mobility can be practised by asking a child to sit on a telephone directory, ensuring that the legs are straight, and encouraging him to reach up for an object with both hands thereby tilting the pelvis.
- Jumping on a trampoline (Fig. 4.16) – the child can also be asked to throw and catch a ball at the same time as jumping (adequate and safe supervision is of paramount importance for all activities related to working on a trampoline).

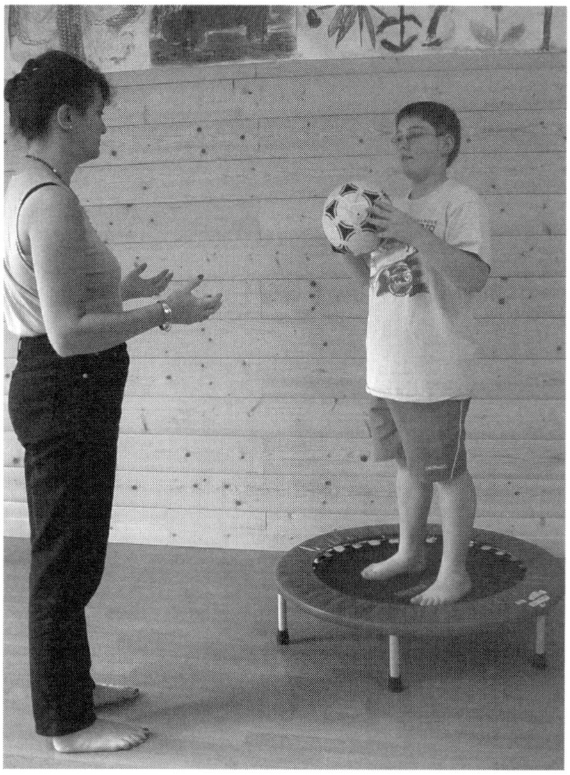

Figure 4.16

- Standing on a wobble board/Sissel cushion or cushion (if balance is poor), bend to pick up a bean bag, stand up and throw into a box (Fig. 4.17).

Figure 4.17

- Sitting on a therapy ball, take the child's weight to each side and forwards and backwards (Fig. 4.18). Time how long the child is able to sit on the ball without falling off.

Figure 4.18

Active trunk extension

- 'Superman throwing balls' (Fig. 4.19). With the child lying on his stomach ask him to throw balls with both hands ensuring that the elbows are raised off the floor and his head is extended. For children who find this difficult, place a pillow under their chest.

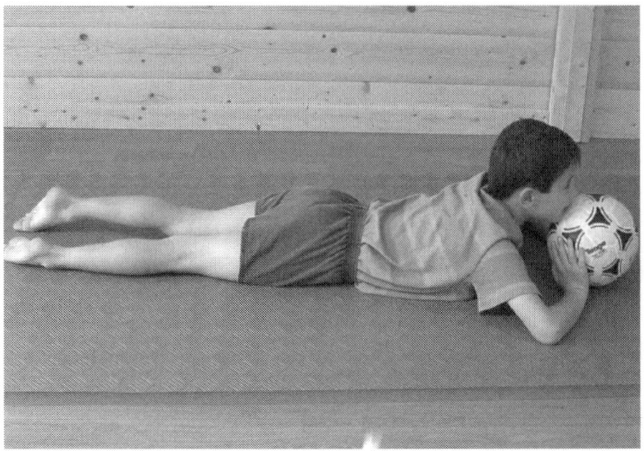

Figure 4.19

- 'The cannon'. Ask the child to lie on his stomach and place his hands down by his side. The child is then asked to lift his head and shoulders off the ground and hold for 2–5 seconds.
- 'The big bounce' (Fig. 4.20). In the standing position, pick up a large therapy ball with both hands from the floor and lift above the head. Turn around and bounce the ball to another person (so throwing the ball from behind the body).

Figure 4.20

- Scooter board (Fig. 4.21). In a prone lying position with the legs extended and off the floor, ask the child to propel himself forwards with his hands (both hands moving together).

Figure 4.21

- 'The crane' (Fig. 4.22). Lying on a therapy ball, roll and reach for a ball or bean bag with two hands and throw into a box.

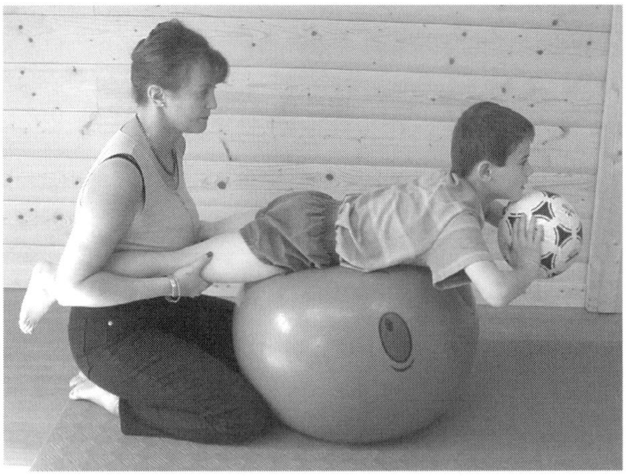

Figure 4.22

- 'Throwing the fruit'. In the four-point kneeling position, ask the child to lift and reach for objects with either hand. He could be asked to reach for a bean bag and throw it into a box.

Active trunk flexion

- 'Head lifts'. Lying on his back with knees flexed and feet on the floor, ask the child to lift his head and hold for count of two.
- 'Knee lifts'. As for the above exercise, but in addition ask the child to lift one knee up to his head and then bring it down again.
- 'Pelvic tilting'. With the child lying on his back with knees bent, he is asked to put his hands into the hollow of his back, tighten his stomach and push down onto his hands.

Rotation

- In the prone lying position, practise reaching up and to the side for objects.
- Practise pivoting in the prone lying position, ensuring that the hips remain in the same position.
- Scooter board activities, especially those involving changing direction.
- Sitting back-to-back with another person and practise passing the ball from side to side.
- Belly dancing.
- Hula hoop.
- In the supine lying position, ask the child to touch with his foot a bean bag which is beside the opposite foot, and then return to the original position.

Eye/hand co-ordination

It is very important when deciding which activities the child should practise that he can succeed at the tasks. For example, if a child is asked to practise throwing and catching tennis balls when he cannot catch them, then self-confidence and self-esteem will deteriorate and he is less likely to want to attempt the tasks. Consider asking the child to use a bean bag first before progressing to a Koosh, followed by a juggling ball and a tennis ball. Children who have difficulty catching bean bags should start with floater balls, balloons or scarves. Activities should be carried out with two hands initially and then progressed to one-handed activities, in particular the dominant hand. The number of repetitions should also be considered, as too many repetitions may result in the child giving up – a good number is considered to be ten attempts, whether or not successful.

- Rolling a ball to another person and making it roll through different-sized tunnels.
- Throwing a balloon or scarf into the air and catching it with two hands.
- Throwing bean bags and different-sized balls into different-sized boxes.
- Bouncing a ball into a hoop which is placed between the child and the therapist.
- Batting a ball either rolling it along the ground or in the air and stopping a rolled ball with a bat.
- Throwing different-sized balls against a wall and catching them, both with and without letting the ball bounce on the floor before catching it.

- Throwing different-sized balls into the air and catching them.
- Bouncing a ball on the floor and catching it.
- As above but ask the child to touch tummy, head, or knee before catching the ball.
- Continuously batting a ball against the wall.

Commercial games

A number of commercial games such as fishing games and mazes are available to assist with eye/hand co-ordination. A list is available from the Dyspraxia Foundation (see Resources for contact details).

Other useful games and activities

- Skittles
- Basketball
- Golf
- Darts
- Tennis
- Badminton
- Table tennis
- Croquet
- Mini golf
- Threading games
- Painting nails
- Peg boards
- Spooning dried peas from one beaker to another
- Pouring water from a jug to a beaker/cup
- Computer games and use of mouse

Figures 4.23 to 4.29 illustrate activities to assist with eye/hand co-ordination.

Figure 4.23

Figure 4.24

Figure 4.25

Figure 4.26

Figure 4.27 Magnetic maze game

Figure 4.28 Magna Force

Figure 4.29 Labyrinth game

Hand exercises

- Wringing out wet towels or flannels
- Scrunching up a small piece of newspaper (A5 size) and, when in a ball, flick it with the index finger on the dominant hand (Figs 4.30 and 4.31).

Figure 4.30

Figure 4.31

- Squeezing soft balls such as squash balls or eggercisers.
- Placing clothes pegs on a line.
- Piano-type games so that individual fingers play a note.
- Cat's cradle (Fig. 4.32)

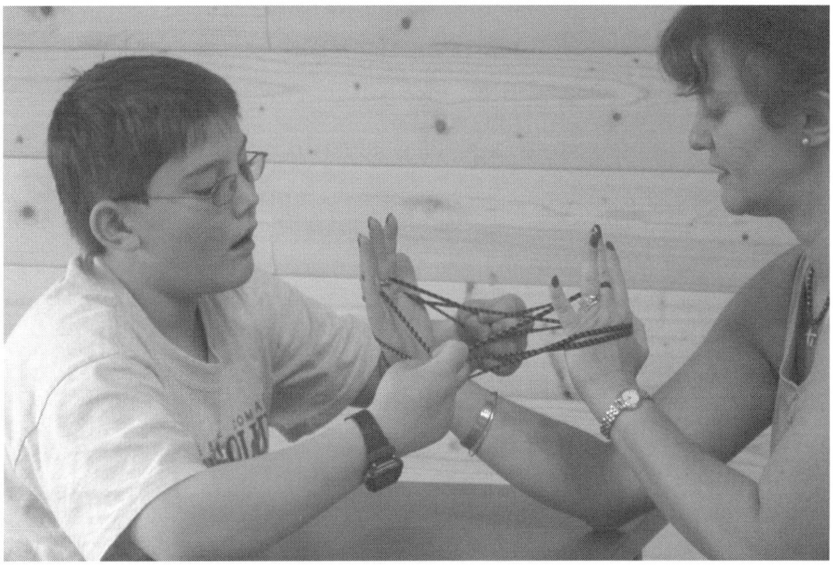

Figure 4.32

- Threading games.
- Peg board games.

- Chopsticks – there is also a commercial game on the market using chopsticks called Chop Stix (Fig. 4.33)

Figure 4.33

Eye/foot co-ordination

- With one foot, touch different objects on the floor.
- Kick a ball against a wall and retrieve it.
- Kick a ball through different-sized tunnels.
- Kick a ball into different-sized goals.
- Dribble a ball along a straight line and in and out of cones.
- Stopping a kicked ball.
- Knocking down skittles by kicking a ball.
- Picking up bean bags with feet.
- Stepping stones, cushions or mats.
- Walking in and out of ladders, boxes and hoops.
- Hopscotch.
- Walking on stilts.

The list of activities and games available from the Dyspraxia Foundation gives suggestions of commercial games that will assist eye/foot co-ordination (see Resources for contact details).

- The Wobbler is an example of an activity for eye/foot co-ordination and balance (Fig. 4.34).

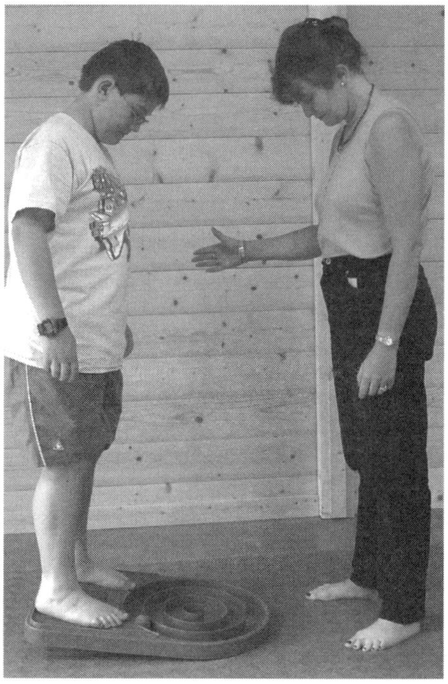

Figure 4.34

- Knocking down skittles by kicking a ball (Fig. 4.35)

Figure 4.35

- Musical floor pianos assist with eye/foot co-ordination, pelvic control, midline crossing, bilateral integration and if hands are used instead of feet, with eye/hand co-ordination (Fig. 4.36).

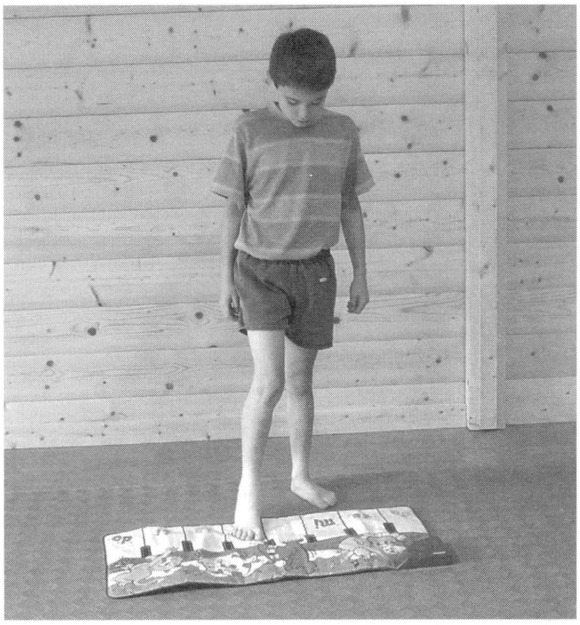

Figure 4.36

- Walking on stilts also assists with bilateral integration and balance (Fig. 4.37).

Figure 4.37

Midline crossing

- Pass objects from one side of the body to the other.
- Throwing and catching balls with two hands diagonally across self.
- Drawing across a page – large figure of eight.
- Reach for objects across self when lying prone.
- When sitting on the floor with legs extended and abducted (legs straight and out to side), practise touching the opposite foot with each hand.
- Kicking balls to opposite corners of a room.
- 'Simon Says' game which involves activities to cross midline.
- Bat and ball games.
- Pathfinder/Button Maze assists with midline crossing as well as planning, short-term visual memory and eye/hand co-ordination (Fig. 4.38).

Figure 4.38

- Twister assists with many skills including midline crossing, eye/foot and eye/hand co-ordination, planning and short-term verbal memory (Fig. 4.39).

Figure 4.39

Directional awareness

- Ball activities.
- In the prone lying position, over the scooter, practise moving in all directions and in and out of cones.
- In activities such as running, skipping and hopping, practise moving in all directions.
- Floor maps and mazes.
- Obstacle courses – moving through tunnels, under tables in different directions.
- Map reading.
- Throwing and bouncing ball games and moving forwards, sideways and backwards.
- Moving in and out of obstacles with the scooter board or with scooters.

Spatial awareness

- Obstacle courses.
- Going in, out and over obstacles, furniture, etc. and moving within the environment.
- Pouring games.
- Hand ball games.
- Stepping over skittles or stepping into and out of boxes.
- Trampoline work.
- Stick in the mud and rescuing another member by going through their legs.

Bilateral integration

- Walking sideways with feet pointing forwards.
- Individual jumps to the side.
- Rolling within two ropes.
- Pedalling bicycle or tricycle.
- Moving around a room using a scooter.
- Labyrinth game.
- Scissor jumps on a trampoline.
- Threading beads.
- Bouncing therapy or large ball with alternate hands as in basketball.

Symmetrical integration

- With both hands rolling a large ball away and stopping it when it is returned.
- Jumping from one spot to another with both feet landing together and stopping in between each jump.
- Jumping on a trampoline with both feet landing together and jumping astride and together.
- Continuously bouncing a ball with both hands together (as in basketball) with a large ball or football.
- Sitting on the floor, bending both knees and kicking a ball away with both feet together.

- Jumping with a space hopper – this also assists with balance.

Figure 4.40

Knowledge of the two sides

- Place coloured stickers on the hands in order for the child to discriminate between the left and right side.
- Teach the child that he 'writes with his right hand' or 'he can make an L-shape with his left thumb and index finger' to discriminate between the right and left.
- Place a set of coloured balls into one box and repeat the task with another set of coloured balls with the other hand.
- Games such as Twister that give instructions for right or left side.
- For children who have a dominance but a tendency to use either hand, ensure that all hand and ball activities are predominantly played with the dominant hand.
- Shake child's hand on arrival, greeting him/her with 'Hello Mr/Mrs right hand'.

Rhythm and timing

- Using a drum, beat it fast and slowly and ask the child to move accordingly, i.e. walk for a slow beat and run for fast; stop moving when the beats stop.
- 'Pat a Cake' and other clapping hand games.
- Bouncing ball activities to self with either or both hands and count at same time.
- Dancing.

Body perception and proprioception

- 'Simon Says' – touch parts of the body to order.
- 'Angels in the snow'. When lying supine with eyes open, move one or more limbs to order. This can be repeated with eyes closed.
- Twister game.
- Obstacle courses.
- Copying mirrored movements.
- Dressing with eyes closed.

- Weight-bearing activities such as crab walking.
- Identifying body parts with eyes closed.

Visual and auditory interpretation

Visual

- Copying designs with cubes, pegs and beads.
- Memory games using groups of familiar objects which must be memorised and then named.
- Copying single motor tasks when demonstrated to the child.
- What is the difference? Looking at two pictures and noting the difference between them.
- Looking at a picture which is then removed and asking the child questions about the picture.
- Kim's game (Fig. 4.41). The child is shown items which are then removed – he must remember all the items.

Figure 4.41

- Obstacle courses – demonstrating the course without saying anything to the child.
- Electronic games such as Match Me and other computer games (Fig. 4.42).

Figure 4.42

- Retail memory games such as Pairs and Snap (Fig. 4.43).

Figure 4.43

- Repeating verbally the sequences of activities shown to the child before completing the activities.

Auditory

- Carry out simple commands of motor sequences. (*Note*: record the number of commands but remember that selecting a colour or object is also a command, e.g. place the **red beanbag in** the **box** uses four choices for one sequenced command.)
- Obstacle courses – verbally tell the child the sequences of the course.
- Listening to a story and asking the child simple questions about it.
- Listening to sounds outside and naming the sounds heard.
- Using a set of shakers which have a pair of sounds and asking the child to find the matching pairs.
- Repeating a list of words or numbers.
- Repeating a list of words or numbers but in the reverse order.
- Listen to two lists of four or five words with the second list missing one word from the original list. Ask the child to state which word was missing from the second list.
- Reciting games such as 'When I went shopping I bought . . .'
- Repeating verbally the tasks asked of him before carrying them out.

Gross motor sequencing

- Practise a few activities at a time, i.e. two or three tasks at a time.
- Simple obstacle courses.
- Ask the child to reverse the sequence of the completed course or task.
- Progress by adding number and direction to the sequences and increasing the number of tasks.

Kinaesthesia

- Practise copying arm actions from the therapist (mirror image after standing behind the therapist).
- Feely boxes.
- Twister.

Gross motor planning

- Obstacle courses.
- Twister.
- Dressing and undressing.
- 'Follow the Leader' and 'Simon Says' games.
- Under and over games – tunnels, hoops, chairs.
- Climbing frames.

Self-organisational skills

- Dressing/undressing – have clothes laid out in order. Get clothes ready the night before.
- Job lists of daily activities such as getting school things ready, brushing teeth, etc.

Table 4.4 Daily job list

	Monday	*Tuesday*	*Wednesday*	*Thursday*	*Friday*	*Saturday*	*Sunday*
Make bed							
Brush teeth							
Wash face							
Get school things ready							
Do physiotherapy exercises							
Do homework							

- Cooking – following recipes, making sandwiches, preparing and working out the timing for roast lunch; preparing the list and getting the bag ready for items needed for swimming, football practice or spending the night away from home. Ask the child to verbally explain before completing the task.
- Preparing a picnic basket.
- Revising for examinations – those children with good visual memory should be encouraged to use colour-coded cards with pictures to depict topics and use highlighters to emphasise a point. For those children who have good verbal memory, encouragement should be given to discussion of the topics and recording the information onto a tape which they can play back.

- Sort out drawers in their room so that each drawer has a particular item in it such as T-shirts in one, shorts in another, etc. and label them.
- Children should be encouraged to use box files for each subject, in which a text book and writing book can be kept together for each subject. Different-coloured boxes help the child to differentiate subjects.
- Using Post-it notes in order to write down things to remember to do or to take into school.
- Giving the child a watch with an alarm to help him to remember to attend special lessons.
- Using a town floor-map to help direct the child to get from one place to another. Reverse the exercise so the child directs you.
- Map reading:
  - ask the child to recite how to get somewhere that is familiar to him such as going to school and give landmarks of places he would pass or how he would know where to turn (e.g. I turn left at the postbox)
  - use his fingers to follow and plan a route from one town to another
  - ask the child to name the towns that he would pass
  - ask the child to name the numbers of the main roads, e.g. A40, A412.
  - ask the child how to get back to the original town.
- Planning stories using a spider's web.

Key points to consider:

Key character:	**Other characters:**	**Key questions to ask yourself**
• his/her name • what they looked like • their character	• their names • what they looked like • their character	• **what** happens? • **who** does it happen to? • **when** does it happen? • **how** does it happen? • **where** does it happen?

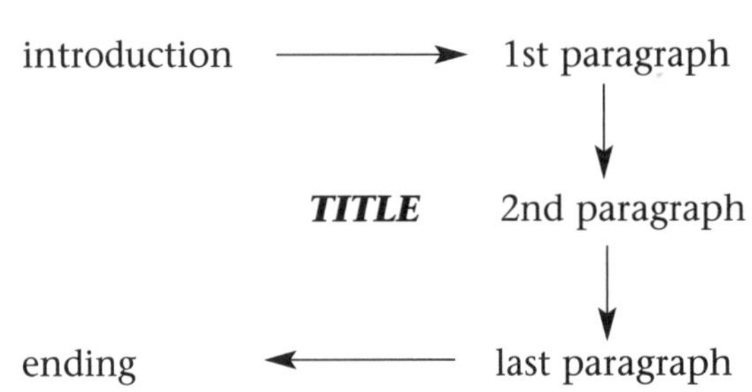

Figures 4.44 to 4.46 illustrate examples of commercial games to assist with self-organisational skills, sequencing, planning and short-term memory.

A number of these commercial games are available which assist with organisational and planning activities; a list of games is available from the Dyspraxia Foundation (see Resources for contact details).

Figure 4.44 Downfall

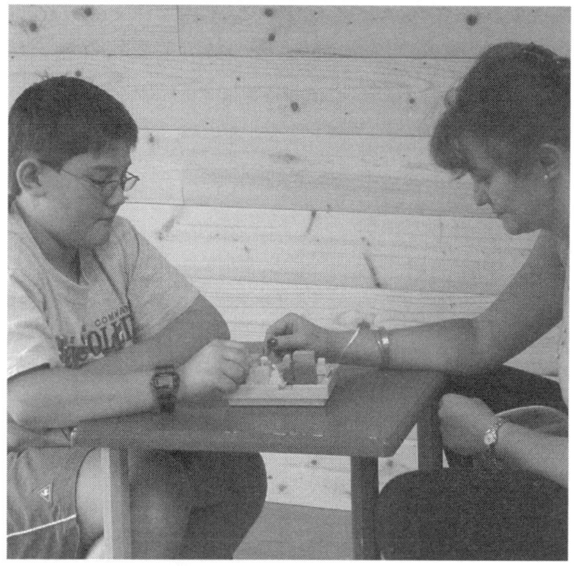

Figure 4.45 Rush hour

Figure 4.46 Go-getter

Strategies for a child moving into secondary school

- Learn the names of teachers and the subjects they teach prior to starting.
- Make a map of the school and learn it – make a special note of where and how to get to the lockers, the dining room and any other important classrooms.
- Obtain a plastic box file for each subject to hold the file/exercise book and text book. Use different colours for each subject and mark them with your name and the subject on the outside.
- At the end of each week take home all the files to sort out, ensuring that any spare sheets are placed in the correct subject file.
- Ensure you have enough pens, pencils, colouring pencils, rulers, rubbers, mathematical equipment, calculator and sharpeners before each term starts. Each weekend, check you have all the items you need.
- Use a brightly coloured pencil case or one that you can easily distinguish as yours and mark it with your name.
- Make 3–4 copies of your timetable and homework timetable and keep one at home. Keep spare copies in your locker, school bag and in a pocket. Laminate them to protect them from possible damage.
- Keep any keys carefully attached to you. Ensure you have spare copies for home and one for the school.
- Aim to arrive at school early so that you can get out the files needed for the morning lessons and any other equipment that may be needed.
- At lunch times give yourself enough time (five minutes at least) to prepare everything that will be needed for the afternoon lessons.
- Check your watch before each lesson to ensure that you arrive on time. **Keep to the five-minute rule** – be five minutes early before each lesson, especially at the start of the day and after breaks. This will give you time to:
  - get out pencils, pens, etc. before the start of the lesson;
  - ensure you have your books ready.
- Keep a small exercise book in your pocket so that any extra notes that you need to remember can be written down.
- Check these notes at the end of the day.
- Use a homework diary to write down your homework and when it needs to be handed in. Use a calendar to write down when assignments need to be handed in.
- Ensure at the end of the day you do not rush home:
  - check your homework timetable and make sure you have all the books you need to take home;
  - make sure you understand what you have to do for the homework;
  - take home any other items, e.g. sports bag for washing etc.;
  - make sure your locker is tidy.
- Keep a list of items that need to be taken home at the weekend.

LOCKER LIST

- Get out the files I need for my classes today.
- Hand in any homework due in today.
- Is my locker tidy?
- Have I written down all instructions for homework?
- What items do I need to take home tonight?
- Are there any messages or notes to be taken home?

Stamina and endurance

- Trampolining.
- Step-ups.
- Press-ups.
- Walking/cycling/jogging.
- Swimming.
- Obstacle courses.
- Skipping.
- Space hopper.

Self-confidence and self-esteem

- Give praise and positive encouragement as much as possible.
- Encourage teachers and parents to give positive encouragement.
- Consider using reward systems such as stars for good work.
- Show the child examples of his progress as often as possible.

- Always carry out tasks that the child can achieve, e.g. when throwing and catching use a bean bag initially and then progress to juggling balls and tennis balls when you know he will be able to manage it – never set tasks that are too difficult.
- Ask the child to write down all the good things about himself and keep this where he can see it to refer back to.

Additional ideas for group therapy

Many of the activities listed above may be used in a group situation. Some examples of these plus other activities that may be carried out are given below.

Warm-up period

- Introduction games such as 'My name is ... and I am throwing the ball to ...' may also be played using a parachute and swapping places or kicking a ball.
- Tag games: one person is IT and when another person is caught they become IT – different themes can be adopted such as using a hat or Wellington boot which is worn by IT.
- Dodge ball using soft balls and two teams who have to throw balls at the opposing team. When the ball touches a person then that member of the team is out.
- Stuck in the mud: one person is IT and has to catch the people – to be freed another person has to go through his/her legs.
- Musical bumps or chairs.

Cooling down

- Sleeping lions: children lie on the floor and stay as still as possible. When they are seen to move they are out.
- Chinese whispers: everyone sits in a line – the first person makes up a short sentence and whispers it to the next person and the message is sent down the line. The last person must state the message.
- Duck Duck Goose: everyone forms a circle. One person designated IT walks around the group touching each person's head saying 'Duck . . . duck' and when 'goose' is said the person touched must get up and chase IT. The first person back to the space sits down and the person standing starts again.

Games for stamina

- Circuits with step-ups, bunny hops and jumping.
- Team games with races using space hoppers, sack races, changing clothes, scooters.
- Throwing medicine balls to the group.
- Crab football.
- Soft ball rounders.
- Tag games.
- Parachute games.
- Kneel-walking races.

Games for co-ordination

(The following may be done individually or in teams.)

- Kicking balls around cones and into goals.
- Batting balloons along the length of a room or in and out of cones.
- Dribbling small balls with a hockey stick around a room.
- Walking on stilts.
- Throwing bean bags or balls to each other and catching.
- Egg and spoon races.
- Bouncing therapy balls around a room.
- Other games include rounders, netball and football.

Planning/organising and memory activities

- In two teams, build obstacle courses for the other team to negotiate.
- In pairs, draw two identical pictures and use these as Pairs.
- In groups, make up marble mazes.
- In groups, explain how to make sandwiches, pack for the weekend, lay the table for a meal.
- Make a map of their room or house.
- Make a map of how to get to school.
- Basic cooking such as making up sandwiches for lunch, making simple cakes such as chocolate crisp cakes.
- Kim's game (see Fig. 4.41).
- Tell a story – one person starts the story and then each person takes a turn to make up and tell one sentence of the story.
- Make up train tracks or road tracks.
- Treasure hunts.

Fine motor skills: treatment

Thorough assessment should have revealed the source of the difficulty that ultimately interferes with function. Probable factors (or a combination of them) may be:

- low tone
- poor shoulder girdle stability
- generalised arm/hand weakness
- poor development of grips, e.g. palmar grasp – superior forefinger grip
- poor tactile awareness
- poor proprioception (awareness of movement)
- poorly developed hand specialisation
- reduced ability to achieve individual finger movements
- bilateral co-ordination
- midline crossing

Fine motor ability is necessary for both unilateral (one-handed) and bilateral (two-handed) activities. Bilateral skills require that one hand (dominant) carries out the major manipulation while the other has the role of the assistor/stabiliser. Few children are competently ambidextrous and those with the tendency to swap need encouragement to develop a 'doing' hand and a 'helping' hand in order to develop good functional ability, especially in two-handed tasks, e.g. management of cutlery, buttons, etc. As a precursor to working on the finer hand/finger movements, any other contributing area of possible difficulty must first be addressed.

Finger awareness, isolated movements and tactile discrimination

- Tactile boxes filled with rice, pasta and foam pieces. Hide small objects to find – exclude vision.
- Feely bags – name objects, placed in a bag, by feel. Place objects in the child's pocket to be identified by feel.
- Dab a spot of hand cream on each finger in turn, rub in with thumb.
- Finger puppets – child tries to move each puppet to talk. Try 'kissing' each thumb puppet.
- Keyboards, calculators, computer games.
- 'Simon Says' finger games.
- Finger game songs – commercially available.

Finger strength

- Putty – silly putty, Playdoh, clay-making kits. Poking fingers in, whole-hand squeezing, pinching small pieces off, make a sausage shape that can then be wrapped around the fingers – pull it apart.
- Sticky tape – wrap around finger and thumb (sticky side out), press together/pull apart.
- Collect a variety of different-sized screw-top jars to store small beads, pegs, etc. Practise opening and closing.
- Rubber bands – around fingers to stretch against.

Pinch grip (to tip of index only and/or index and middle)

- Peg boards.
- Hama beads – construction kits that can be ironed together to make a planned shape.
- Straws/sticks cut about 2cm long of a diameter that will fit into peg board holes. Place in the board, pick up, turn over and replace into the hole (now upside down).
- Posting coins into a money box.
- Removing objects from a container with an opening that only fits thumb and index.
- Paper/pencil tug of war – hold in fingertips to be pulled away by another.
- Push pegs into Playdoh or putty to make a hedgehog – pull out.

In-hand manipulation

- Pick up and hold small coins (1p/5p) in palm of hand, collect as many as possible without dropping. Try to collect from the palm with the fingertips to put in a purse.

- Putty – having pinched putty apart into small pieces, collect all and mould back into one whole by repeatedly turning and squeezing without using other hand or pressing onto table.
- Paper scrunching – tear paper into manageable pieces, squeeze together again only using one hand without help from body or table. Can be used for targeting.

Bilateral

- Threading cards – commercially available.
- Threading beads, e.g. jewellery-making kits.
- Nuts and bolts of varying size, e.g. Brio mechanic.
- Construction toys, e.g. Lego/Duplo, KNex, Zocketts, Constructa-straws.

Handwriting: treatment

Handwriting must begin with good pre-writing where the child is helped to develop:

- good overall motor control;
- fine motor control of hand and fingers;
- visual control – eye/hand;
- spatial control – of one's body in space which leads on to an awareness of directionality, horizontal–vertical, side–side and how to transfer this to paper.

The older the child, the more progressively difficult it is to alter their bad habits – particularly with regard to poor grip and incorrect writing movement. Most children seen for handwriting remediation have a combination of problems that result in the writing process remaining at a mechanical stage. Problems range from total illegibility to reasonable legibility but without speed. The lack of automatic ability in writing will 'stunt' creative ability. The child may therefore be able to produce either good writing or good content – but not both.

General considerations in the treatment of handwriting

- Furniture of a suitable height to allow feet to be flat on the floor with the desktop 2in above a bent elbow.
- The forearm should be close to the body to allow good lining up of the wrist with the pencil.
- The wrist should be in a mid-position, the hand and forearm supported on the table. This should result in the hand being maintained under the line/work and not to the side (which necessitates the whole arm being moved away from the work).
- The non-writing hand should be used to stabilise the paper.
- Paper position: when right-handed the paper should slant at the top about 25 degrees to the left, and when left-handed it should slant at the top about 30 degrees to the right.
- Pressure – excessive pressure is common and the following can be tried to alleviate it:
  - increase proprioceptive awareness by squeezing a small, soft foam ball
  - when holding the pencil in a good tripod grip, use the other hand in a pull/push motion so that the writing hand has to hold on tightly
  - place a piece of carbon paper between the work and an extra piece of paper and ask the child to write so that an impression does *not* go through to the paper underneath

The LEFT-handed writer

- They should not be placed in the class with a right-hander on their left.
- The forearm should be out and away from their body.
- The non-writing hand should not only stabilise the paper but should be used to help 'feed' the paper as the writing progresses across the page.
- Paper needs careful placement as described above with the hand working under the line to avoid a hooked grip.

Useful equipment

- Sloping boards – encourage upright posture, better hand/eye position and ocular-motor control. Can be home-made (providing a slope of 20 degrees) or bought from Philip & Tacey or Back in Action (see Resources for contact details).
- Handhugger pencils – useful in the *development* of good tripod grip but may not be sufficient to correct an already established poor grip.
- Corrective commercially available grips:
  - ordinary tripod – of little corrective benefit
  - Stubbi/Stetro grips – specific tripod finger placement, difficult for the younger child, can be incorrectly applied (Taskmaster, see Resources for contact details)
  - Ultra pencil grip – recently arrived from the USA, large and comfortable, same application for right/left (Taskmaster)
  - Start right – only available from the USA, barrier prevents thumb wrap and low pencil/pen hold (OT ideas, see Resources for contact details).

It is often useful to obtain a small sample of different pencils and pens for children to try before parents are advised to buy. Many commercial companies (Pentel, Parker, Schneider, Lamy and Schaefer) supply pencils and pens with grips that may help the child. Some children prefer rubber grips to ensure that their fingers do not slip. Faber-Castell produce the Grip 2001, a small tripod pencil with a grip zone which has proved successful with many children. Pencil grips need careful prescription and regular supervision of use to be effective.

- Masking tape strips can be used on the table as a guide to paper placement.
- Pens – for older children who need to make the transition to ink pens some experimentation will be required. Fountain pens are rarely successful, especially if control of pressure is an issue – the nib is easily damaged and affects control. Alternatives to try include: Berol handwriting pen, Stabilo S' move, Schreiber refillable roller ball, Pilot retractable G-2 07 gel pen. Stypen roller ball also manufacture a fountain pen with an indented grip.
- Lined paper (the size of line gap is determined by the size of the child's writing) supports improvement of perceptual-motor control.

Commercially available handwriting programmes

- *Handwriting Without Tears* by Jan Olsen (available from the Psychological Corporation, see Resources for contact details). Good early years, teaches good habits, ideas for 'readiness', right/left discrimination and avoidance of reversals.
- *Write Start* (Teodorescu) by Lois Addy (available from the Dyspraxia Foundation, see Resources for contact details). Perceptual-motor approach, photocopiable programme, spans a good age range, gives supplemental activity ideas to support each stage.
- *The Handwriting File* by J. Alston and J. Taylor (1984). A complete resource for evaluation and treatment including teaching ideas on specific components.

Any early years writing programmes that practise correct start/finish points support good habit formation and make the transition to cursive easier. Practise of pre-writing patterns on a vertical surface, e.g. blackboard, whiteboard or large sheets of paper, regularly revisited, can help increase 'flow' of writing and control of directional change.

Effective handwriting treatment needs to follow critical assessment and is best carried out by an experienced occupational therapist. Programmes can rarely be generalised and must be specific to the needs of each child. Consideration should be given to the following as influencing factors:

- The writing style of the school.
- The demands made at school relative to the child's age.
- The amount of time available at home and school for supervised practice. Regular short periods are preferable, e.g. ten minutes at a time.
- The commitment of the school to implementing strategies/changes or to allow alternative means of recording (early access to keyboarding skills may be recommended).

Reviews

Reviews should follow treatment to ensure that the progress made is maintained. Initially a review should be available three months following completion of the treatment. The original assessment should be used as a comparison in order to ascertain the improvements. Parents should also be given the opportunity to outline the progress the child has made with activities of daily living within the home and school environment. The effectiveness of treatment can also be determined at this time by reviewing the goals and aims of treatment as well as by using other tools such as outcome measures (this will be discussed further in the following chapter).

Annual reviews offer an ideal opportunity to ensure that the child and his family are happy with his abilities and progress. As the child enters adolescence, new problems may become apparent such as social skills, sitting examinations, looking after himself (shaving etc.). These can be identified and appropriate help and advice given.

Treatment recording

It is crucial that all treatment sessions are recorded accurately and legibly. Charts that list the main exercises are a quick and easy method of recording the number of repetitions completed. These can then be reviewed at a glance to see how the child has progressed. Parents can be encouraged to complete the record sheets. This helps the parents to join in with the session and to monitor improvements at the same time. Space should be made available (at the bottom of the sheets) for the therapist to record her own findings, sign and date them (Appendix 3).

Outside activities

Once treatment has been completed, it becomes more important that children should be encouraged to get involved in out-of-school activities in order to assist with maintaining their improved muscle strength and skills. Generally, no more than two extra activities should be recommended per week so that the child still has time to relax and carry out his school work. Sport introduced at an appropriate time may be enjoyed for a lifetime and it should be remembered that leisure time should be fun. It is important that parents are guided by their children's own levels of enthusiasm and that pressure is not placed upon the child to reach a certain standard in a set time by a far-from-sympathetic teacher (Cocks 1996). Activities could include tennis, swimming, football, karate/judo, rowing, basketball, chess, Scouts, horse-riding and cycling. Clubs also offer very good training where skills are practised; these can assist the child with social skills. The club should not necessarily expect the child to compete in fixtures against other clubs but it should allow him to join in the training sessions.

In addition, other hobbies can be encouraged that do not require children to become involved in competitive sports. These will provide an outside interest and assist with social skills. Hobbies such as starting a collection, keeping pets, cooking, fishing, music, computer studies, drama club, gardening and photography are good examples.

The Dyspraxia Foundation has local groups, some of which offer clubs and activities for children. These are beneficial in that they allow the child the opportunity to attempt new tasks in a safe and understanding environment. In addition, some local sports centres also provide groups for children with difficulties and this allows them to compete against other children with similar problems. Many therapists are now being asked to give advice and input into these groups so that the children's needs are suitably addressed.

Care should be taken when recommending sports and activities – although swimming is an ideal way of providing movement through a different medium, some children with sensory defensiveness may not like noise, splashing or being on a slippery surface. They may be very slow at dressing and may not enjoy the prospect of swimming. Children who have gravitational insecurity (dislike heights and do not like taking their feet off the floor) may have difficulty getting into the water. Once in the water they then cannot cope with the range and freedom of movement if they are not able to control the rate and speed of their movement. Other sports may also need to be carefully considered. For example, children who are afraid of heights may find sitting on a horse threatening.

Adventure playgrounds

Adventure playgrounds present the child with a challenging, yet fun, environment in which he can attempt new skills or just stay with the old ones until he feels confident and safe enough to be more ambitious and to extend his skills further.

For children who are very impetuous, this area is not as safe as soft play and parents and teachers should be aware of the dangers.

Soft play adventure playgrounds may well be less threatening to the child and provide a safer environment. These playgrounds are not ideal if crowded with other children – this environment may too noisy for the child and there is the risk of the child being pushed over.

Holiday workshops

Holiday workshops are very beneficial for the children once treatment has been completed. They can be used as a way of allowing children who have been treated on an individual basis to work in a group situation, to continue to practise the skills they have developed and learnt, as well as an opportunity for the therapists to see how the children are progressing. It is also an opportunity for parents to meet each other. They can be combined with a number of other therapies such as physiotherapy, occupational therapy, art therapy and music therapy to add variety and offer development of other skills. Giving the workshops themes such as 'Big Eggscape' (Easter) often provides a fun element – especially if games can be tailored to fit the theme!

Workshops aim to further develop:

- co-ordination skills;
- short-term memory skills;
- stamina and endurance;
- planning and organisational skills;

- fine motor skills;
- social skills;
- empowerment;
- creative skills.

How parents can help

Parents play a vital role in the development and support of their child. The list below details some important advice:

- Realise that it is not your fault that your child has difficulties!
- Remember the importance of providing lots of encouragement and positive feedback to your child.
- Work out ways to help your child when revising, remembering things for school, doing homework, special lessons or jobs. The use of reminders, Post-it notes and other strategies described under 'Self-organisational skills' may be useful.
- Give support and encouragement to your child while completing the home programmes by ensuring that there is adequate time allowed for the programme and by making it as much fun as possible.
- Remember the importance of additional sports and activities in order to maintain muscle strength and assist with social skills and concentration as well as reducing stress for the child and maintaining and improving the cardiac and respiratory systems.
- Find out about good games to assist with areas such as eye/hand co-ordination, short-term memory, planning and organisational skills (the Dyspraxia Foundation has useful leaflets, see Resources for contact details).
- Parents often need support themselves and support groups such as the Dyspraxia Foundation will be able to put you in touch with local groups and contacts.
- Children do not like change and so being consistent is important; try to keep items in the same place and, during the holidays, tell the child the daily plans at the beginning of the day.
- Extra guidance may be needed as the child progresses from adolescence into adulthood and advice may be required for activities such as organising himself in the home (e.g. cooking, cleaning), studying, working and communications and relationships (see Colley 2000 for good advice).

Advice for teachers

Many teachers have had very little experience of working with children with dyspraxia and some may still not have heard of the condition. It is therefore important to advise and inform the teacher – and, indeed, the school – of the condition. Teachers will need to be given advice on helping the child within both the classroom and the PE setting. Often a small leaflet describing the condition, what to look for, what treatment involves and some useful hints for the classroom situation is helpful. The Dyspraxia Foundation's professional section, which supports and provides information for the medical and educational professions, has produced leaflets with suggested activities for PE and advice for the classroom (useful for school libraries). Information on suitable games, hobbies and activities to assist the child will all be helpful. You may find the following advice useful:

- Be aware of and understand the child's difficulties. He will have problems carrying out instructions and it may appear that he is not listening when in fact he cannot remember the tasks he has been given. Ask the child to repeat the instructions and keep them simple –never give too many at one time.

- These children are very easily distracted so consideration should be given to where they sit in the classroom, i.e. not near windows/doors or at a table with children who could easily distract them. In addition, they often have difficulty with hearing so they should be positioned close to you so that they can hear instructions as well as see the board.
- A good sitting posture is important – sitting upright with the feet flat on the floor.
- Seek advice on the most appropriate pencils and pens to use.
- These children also tire quickly and have poor stamina. Concentration spans are short so ensure that this is accommodated within the lessons. As many of the children are unable to sit for long periods, time should be made available to allow the child to walk around the classroom. As a start, allow the child to stand up every 5–10 minutes – less often as the child progresses and improves.
- You should be able to give advice on strategies to help the child such as how to remember homework (e.g. prep diary) and how to write essays.
- Teachers also need advice and support so close liaison with the therapist is important.
- Be aware that it is important that the child should be able to join in with as many activities and games lessons as possible. Ensure that he has the skills that are required for the sports, e.g. in football, if he is placed in goal he needs to have sufficient eye/hand as well as eye/foot co-ordination for the position.
- Problems may manifest themselves repeatedly or different problems may become apparent as the child grows into adolescence. Further advice and/or treatment may be required at this time.

In addition, close liaison with the class teacher during treatment is recommended as this will ensure that any difficulties encountered in the classroom can be resolved. It is also helpful for the teacher to know how the child is progressing during treatment and the specific areas that are being addressed. A liaison diary, which is taken between therapist and teacher by the parent, may work well as this will allow all those involved with the child to communicate the necessary information to each other. Many schools welcome summary assessments and progress reports on the child.

Private sector

Many parents turn to the private sector due to long waiting lists and the apparent shortage of therapists under the National Health Service (NHS). Therapists willing to see patients privately should ensure that they are covered adequately for insurance purposes and should follow the guidelines as set out by their professional bodies. Parents should check their insurance policy if they wish to claim. Therapists must be aware that they may need to be registered with the insurance company as a provider.

As cover differs between the various policies, parents should be asked to contact their own insurance company to ensure they are covered for the necessary treatment and to determine the referral system required (i.e. can the child be referred by the parent or is a referral by a GP/consultant needed?). It should be remembered that the contract for treating the child is between the parent and the therapist so it is advisable to request payment from the parents at the time of consultation (they then make a claim against their insurance company). This will prevent long delays in reimbursement and/or unnecessary paperwork and difficulties.

Parents in turn must ensure that the therapist is state registered and uses medically recognised forms of treatment. They should also ask for information concerning the effectiveness of the treatment used by the therapist.

Further advice concerning setting up a practice should be obtained from professional bodies.

Chapter 5

The Effectiveness of Treatment

Definition of effectiveness

> Effectiveness is the quality of being able to accomplish something. (*Shorter Oxford Dictionary*)

Proving the effectiveness of any treatment is becoming an integral part of our working lives. It is therefore important that the therapist has a clear understanding of what she has an effect on and how she can prove her treatment is effective.

The importance of involving the parents in the setting of goals has been discussed and these form a useful tool for ascertaining the effectiveness of treatment, especially from the parents' subjective viewpoint. An objective score of the improvement made by the child will be shown by the use of objective standardised assessments.

Treatment will have an effect on:

- gross motor skills;
- ball skills;
- fine motor/manual dexterity;
- activities of daily living;
- self-confidence and self-esteem.

Completing audit and research studies will allow the therapist to evaluate and improve on the treatment given. Some of the studies on both group therapy and individual treatment are discussed below.

Norton and Twentyman (1995) considered the effect of group therapy on children with co-ordination problems. The group, which met for a six-week period after school, was divided during each session into gross motor skills, perception, ball skills and fine motor ability. No assessment was made on pre- and post-treatment scores, but the authors concluded that 'it is more efficient and effective to treat children in groups rather than individually or simply to provide a programme of therapy'. They also stated that 'children see the groups as clubs; they enjoy attending and succeed in physical activities, sometimes for the first time'. Parents also reported the value of the groups. The authors, however, decided that in order to further prove their work, specific aims and objectives would have to be set and that utilising standardised tests and questionnaires would improve standards and objectivity.

Addy (1996) used the Movement ABC Assessment Battery at the beginning and end of treatment to evaluate the effect of a joint physiotherapy and occupational therapy programme. Specific standards and goals were set for the programme which consisted of three 6–7-week courses in rebound therapy, aquacise and perceptual/proprioceptive stimulation carried out in weekly group sessions for one hour after school. Each child attended a minimum of two terms and a few attended for more than two years. The results showed that scores improved after treatment in all but one child.

Lee and Smith (1998) used outcome measures (devised by Lee *et al.* for the Association of Paediatric Chartered Physiotherapists) to score improvements in gross motor skills following treatment. A total of 60 children were treated on an individual basis for eight weekly sessions which was supplemented by a daily home programme of activities and exercises. Scores showed that by the end of the eight-week block of treatment each child, on average, made an improvement of 69 per cent. By the review (three months later) each child on average had improved their scores to 73 per cent. Parents similarly reported an improvement of 72 per cent in those activities they had wished to see improve (such as writing, running, dressing, eating). Lee and Smith concluded that long-term monitoring of the children was needed in order to ensure that progress was maintained.

Williams *et al.* (1999) studied the effects of a physiotherapy intervention programme which consisted of a ten-week course of group therapy. Each session lasted 45 minutes and was supplemented by a daily home programme. The ABC movement test was used to measure the changes. All children were reported to have made significant improvement, especially with ball skills and motor co-ordination, although no change was noted with manual dexterity. It was considered that this was due to emphasis being placed on ball skills and gross motor patterns rather than on fine motor skills. As a result of their findings, an occupational therapist has since joined the group and each course has been extended to 12 weeks to include work on fine motor skills.

Lee and Smith (2002) carried out a three-year study on the progress of children following physiotherapy treatment for dyspraxia. Of the 60 children who were in the original study, 33 had continued to attend for reviews. In total, 12 children had required a further course of treatment, all of whom had experienced a sudden growth spurt prior to the further course. All the children had then continued to maintain, if not improve upon their scores (the original study scores compared with those at the reviews). In addition, all parents were sent a questionnaire of which 53 (88 per cent) were returned. Parents reported that they were happy with their child's progress especially with gross motor skills, self-confidence and social skills. There were, however, still some concerns voiced about school work, in particular mathematics, writing and short-term memory.

Lee *et al.* (2003) looked at the improvement in self-esteem following physiotherapy treatment: 25 children were assessed to consider their self-esteem levels prior to and after treatment. All the children underwent an eight-week programme of individual treatment carried out on a daily basis and treatment was supplemented by a daily home programme. All the children improved their scores by an average of 3.21 points. Only one child remained in the low rating following treatment (but the treatment had improved his scores by six points). Parents reported that their children appeared to have gained self-confidence and self-esteem, were willing to attempt more activities and join in games with other children. They also were less likely to give up on difficult tasks as previously noted.

Glendenning *et al.* (2003) considered the effects of improving the postural base, stability and visual-motor control on the motor behaviours and learning abilities of dyspraxic children. They studied 19 children aged 6–11 years. The children received therapy, which comprised neuro-postural, proprioceptice and vestibular elements, twice a week for ten weeks which was followed by 12 weeks of twice weekly visual motor control exercises plus a programme of neuro-postural exercises to carry out at home. The children were reassessed at the end of the programme and six months later. The results showed a greater than expected improvement in all areas with the junior group (11 children) also showing improvement with reading and writing skills. The eight children in the infant group also showed an improvement in focus and language. Self-confidence and self-esteem were also reported to have improved. The authors concluded that the results support the view that an efficient, stable postural base and improved oculo-motor control will have a positive effect on the dyspraxic child's ability to learn.

Quigg (2003) carried out a study from a parental satisfaction questionnaire and therapy observation checklists to determine the effectiveness of therapeutic group work, provided jointly by occupational therapy and physiotherapy, to children with co-ordination difficulties. Nine children were seen in two separate groups (of three and six children) on a weekly basis for six weeks, which was supplemented with a home programme. The results showed that following the treatment, the children were more willing to undertake new activities, indicating they had improved self-confidence and self-esteem. Gross motor skills also improved. Parents reported that they found the home programme helpful as it taught them how to work with their child. The therapists, however, concluded that their audit had limitations – the study only looked at a small number of children and the therapy checklist had not been previously piloted – and that a much longer time frame (of 12 weeks) would provide more reliable data.

Lee and Yoxall (2004) considered whether the interests of children with dyspraxia changed following physiotherapy treatment. They studied 20 children with a diagnosis of dyspraxia who received weekly treatment for eight weeks which was supplemented by a daily home programme. Results were taken prior to treatment, at the end of treatment and at the review three months later. The results showed that the likes, hobbies and outside activities had all increased – in particular at the three-monthly review. Out-of-school activities had more than doubled. The authors reported that the results may be accounted for by the fact that the children were more willing to attempt new activities and had improved self-confidence and self-esteem. Many children reported that they now enjoyed and were happy to participate in sports at school, which had not been the case prior to treatment. The number of dislikes did not reduce, however; English and history (involving essay-writing), mathematics, spelling and French featured high on the list. This was attributed to the fact that the children continued to have some difficulties with short-term memory and organisational skills, both of which are required for these subjects.

The use of outcome measures

Standardised assessment tools have already been discussed. Outcome measures have been used in order to prove the effectiveness of treatment. Unlike standardised tests, these measures were not designed to help with diagnosis but to audit the effectiveness of treatment.

The measures, scored as percentages, compare the scores in each area of difficulty taken at the original assessment with those taken at the review. A percentage of change is obtained from each area and an overall percentage of improvement is then made. The maximum improvement that can be obtained from any one area is 100 per cent.

The advantages of the outcome measures are:

- they cover all the areas tested in a physiotherapy assessment;
- they can be applied to a whole age range;
- scores can be easily extracted from a therapist's assessment;
- the scores taken are objective, since scores used are either of time taken or of a number completed by the child;
- results can be used as a guide for determining treatment areas;
- results are measured in percentages which is easy for parents and referrers to understand.

Lee and Smith (1998) described in detail the tests for outcome measures and their findings. Their results, along with the others described in this chapter, only consider the short-term effects of treatment. Lee and Smith (2002), however, followed the progress of 53 children from their original study over a three-year period. Their results showed that the children had maintained their progress following treatment and in many cases they had improved upon their scores. Parents also reported that their children had shown improvement with self-confidence and self-esteem and that they continued to be more willing to participate in and attempt new activities. In addition, their children were more readily accepted by their peers and they found it easier to make friends. Twelve children required a further course of treatment in the first two years of the study. Parents of eight of the children, who had required a further course of treatment, commented that difficulties had become apparent after sudden growth spurts when the children were aged 7–8 years. Following the second course of treatment, all twelve children made good progress with their motor skills. A few parents from the study did report that they continued to have concerns but these were related to school work such as mathematics, spelling and reading and short-term memory.

It is of paramount importance, if therapists are to be effective, that further studies are carried out on the long-term effects of treatment.

Appendix 1: Standardised Tests

Developmental Test of Visual-Motor Integration
(The VMI or Beery Assessment)

Authors K. Beery and N. Buktenica	*Published in* 1989
Age range 2 years 9 months–19 years 8 months	*Time to administer* 10–15 minutes individually or in a group.
Aim To identify visual motor difficulties.	
Advantages • There is evidence to substantiate the fact that scores on the VMI correlate with academic performance in reception years and also predictive reading difficulties.	*Disadvantages* • Scoring criterion is somewhat subjective. • Lack of British standardisation.
Validity/Reliability The test is standardised well (5,824 children) but its 'normative' sample was taken from a limited geographical distribution within North America.	*Supplier* NFER-Nelson, The Chiswick Centre, 414 Chiswick High Road, London W4 5TF (Tel: 0208 996 8444)

Bruininks-Oseretsky Test of Motor Proficiency (BOTMP)

Author	*Published in*
Robert H. Bruininks	1978
Age range 4 years 6 months–14 years 6 months	*Time to administer* 45 to 60 minutes for the complete battery (46 items), 15 to 20 minutes for the short form (14 items).

Aim

To provide a comprehensive picture of a child's motor development. It provides a thorough assessment of the motor proficiency of children with mild to severe motor co-ordination dysfunction. It can serve as a useful basis for developing and evaluating motor training programmes.

It covers eight sub-tests under three specific headings:

a) Gross Motor Development: running speed and agility, balance, bilateral integration, strength (arm, shoulder, abdominal, leg).

b) Gross and Fine Motor Development: upper limb co-ordination.

c) Fine Motor Development: response speed, visual-motor control, upper limb speed and dexterity.

Advantages

- The Bruininks-Oseretsky Test provides a separate measure of gross/fine motor skills making it possible to obtain meaningful comparisons of performance in two areas.
- With the complete battery, it is possible to obtain three composite scores: Gross Motor, Fine Motor and Battery Composite.
- Two forms of test are available for fast screening and more detailed assessment.

Disadvantages

- It aims to measure motor skills relevant to everyday functional activities. Some of the tests, however, do not appear to fit into this category.
- It is possible to fail items as a result of weak perceptual skills rather than dysfunctional motor co-ordination.
- Queries have also arisen regarding age-equivalent scores, particularly in relation to balance and bilateral integration.

Validity/Reliability

Standardisation was based on 765 children selected through stratified sampling. The sample tended to be white and middle-class and was therefore demographically biased. Extreme caution should be applied when using this test with children who are learning disabled because it has not been demonstrated whether their lower performance is due to weak motor skill or to their learning difficulties.

Supplier

NFER-Nelson, The Chiswick Centre, 414 Chiswick High Road, London W4 5TF (Tel: 0208 996 8444)

Peabody Developmental Motor Scales and Activity Scales (PDMS)

Authors M. Rhonda Folio and Rebecca R. Fewell	*Published in* 1983
Age range 0–6 years 11 months	*Time to administer* 45–60 minutes (20–30 minutes per scale).

Aim

Early childhood motor development programme that provides structured motor programmes for gross and fine motor skills. The Gross Motor Scale contains 170 items divided into 17 age levels with 10 items on each level. The Fine Motor Scale contains 112 items divided into 16 age levels with 6 or 8 items on each level.

Advantages • The large number of items provides a greater opportunity for the child to demonstrate his/her motor abilities to the assessor. • It can be used as a criterion-referenced measure of motor patterns and skills. • It is norm-referenced.	*Disadvantages* • Scoring criteria are somewhat subjective. • Lack of British standardisation.
Validity/Reliability The test is standardised well.	*Supplier* Psychological Corporation, 32 Jamestown Road, London NW1 7BY (Tel: 0207 424 4456)

The Movement ABC Battery

(Movement ABC Battery)

Authors	*Published in*
S. Henderson and D. Sugden	1992
Age range	*Time to administer*
4–12 years	20–40 minutes to complete.

Aim

To identify motor development difficulties. There are two parts to the test:
1. The performance assessment which includes 32 items organised into four sets of 8, each set relating to children's ages: a) Band 1: 4–6 years; b) Band 2: 7–8 years; c) Band 3: 9–10 years; d) Band 4: 11–12 years.
The objectives are:
- To preserve the standardised assessment from the TOMI original version, standardised in the USA.
- To enhance the use of the informal checklist.
- To bring the standardised battery together with the checklist to provide a means of progressing from assessment to intervention.

Each series of tests incorporates manual dexterity, ball skills, and static and dynamic balance. Qualitative observations are also encouraged to determine the quality of the movement patterns.
2. Checklist to be completed by a familiar adult.

Advantages	*Disadvantages*
• Identifies and describes impairments of motor function in children. • Provides information on the child's performance in 1:1 or group situations. • The checklist allows for a quick screening of progress in classroom settings. • Provides quantitative evidence based on age norms (based on a representative sample of 1,200 children). • Provides a breakdown of children's strengths/weaknesses in motor skills and their motivation/attitudes. • Guidance as to remediation is offered. • It is relatively quick to administer.	• It does not break down motor skills into the detail which may be required for treatment. • It does not take into account potential perceptual weaknesses which may affect motor performance.
Validity/Reliability	*Supplier*
Initially standardised on 854 Canadian children. Further standardised on 600 children in the UK and Canada.	Psychological Corporation, 32 Jamestown Road, London NW1 7BY (Tel: 0207 424 4456)

Test of Perceptual Skills (Non-Motor)
(TVPS)

Author	*Published in*
M. F. Gardner	1989
Age range	*Time to administer*
Lower Level 4–12 years; Upper Level 13–18 years	Minimum 60 minutes.

Aim

To identify visual perceptual abilities, using non-motor testing. The test measures seven main areas:
1 Visual discrimination
2 Visual memory
3 Visual-spatial relationships
4 Visual form constancy
5 Visual sequential memory
6 Visual figure/ground discrimination
7 Visual closure
The assessment consists of a series of test plates. Each section has 16 items (forms) arranged in progressive difficulty. The forms are chosen to avoid those with which the child may already be familiar.

Advantages

- The child identifies specified shapes on each page. If he fails three responses simultaneously, then the next section is attempted (i.e. the child is not overtly aware that he has failed).
- Scaled scores, perceptual quotients, percentile ranks and perceptual age equivalents are provided.
- Due to the detailed breakdown of the perceptual areas, it is possible to identify the area of perceptual dysfunction which is of greatest influence in hindering the child's level of occupational performance. Thereafter remediation can focus on this area first.

Disadvantages

- Lack of British standardisation.

Validity/Reliability

The test was standardised on a defined norm group (962 children) within the USA.

Supplier

Ann Arbor Publishing, PO Box 1, Belford, Northumberland NE70 7JX (Tel: 01668 214460)

The Goodenough-Harris Draw-a-Man Test

Authors	*Published in*
F. Goodenough and Dale Harris	1963
Age range	*Time to administer*
2 years 9 months–19 years 8 months	No time limit.

Aim

To use figure drawings as a means of measuring the intellect and psychological state of children to a greater or lesser degree. Three drawings are requested: a man, a woman and a portrait. The drawings are made without prompting and the child is encouraged to take his time and include as much detail as possible. The drawings are scored on 144 items (73 for the male drawing and 71 for the female) and points are awarded according to detail, position and proportion. A scoring manual is provided.

Advantages

- It may be used as either a group or individual test. It requires only pencil and paper (no expensive record forms are needed).
- No training is required of the administrator.
- It is suitable for those who do not speak English, it is non-academic and non-verbal.
- It has a fair degree of validity.
- It can determine if a child has a distorted body image.

Disadvantages

- Scoring criterion is somewhat subjective.
- Visual motor integration may also affect quality of drawing human figures.
- Discrepancy in research over whether the test actually measures what it claims.

Validity/Reliability

High.

Supplier

Psychological Corporation, 32 Jamestown Road, London NW1 7BY (Tel: 0207 424 4456)

B/G Steem Scale with Locus of Control items

Authors B. Maines and G. Robinson	*Published in* 1988
Age range 6–14 years	*Time to administer* Approximately five minutes.

Aim

To assess and give ratings of children's self-esteem.
Five categories are assessed:
1. General
2. Academic
3. Physical
4. Family
5. Social

Separate questionnaires are given to boys and girls and to those in junior school (27 questions) and secondary school (35 questions) with Yes and No answers. Score sheets determine the number of correct answers which can then be used to compare against a table of scores to ascertain whether the results are in the very low/low/normal/high/very high group. In addition, a locus of control can be assessed to determine whether the child considers he has control over his life.

Advantages • No training is required of the administrator. • Easy to administer and score. • Simple language for children to understand. • Several aspects of self-esteem included. • Test standardised on British children. • May be used as an indicator of success following intervention.	*Disadvantages* • Answers may vary according to the child's frame of mind on the day. • If parents are present, they may influence the child's answers.
Validity/Reliability The test was standardised on a sample of 3,346 British children.	*Supplier* Lucky Duck Publishing Ltd, Solar House, Station Road, Kingswood, Bristol BS15 4PH (Tel: 0117 947 5150)

Other useful assessments

- Erdhardt Prehension Test
- Sensory Integration Praxis Test (SIPTS)
- Aston Index
- Miller Pre-School Assessment Test
- Test of Auditory Perception
- Gessell
- Survey of Early Childhood Abilities (SECA)

Appendix 2: Questionnaires

CONFIDENTIAL QUESTIONNAIRE FOR PARENTS

I would be grateful if you could please answer the following questions and *return this form in the enclosed SAE as soon as possible.* This will enable us to ascertain some of your child's problems without asking awkward questions in front of your child which might embarrass either yourself or your child.

Thank you

Re:
Of:
DOB:
Telephone:
Parents' mobile no:

SCHOOL NAME	
Address	
Telephone:	**Class teacher:**
Head teacher:	**PE teacher:**

It is the department's policy to send schools a copy of the summary and a letter explaining how to help your child in the classroom setting.

If you do NOT wish this to take place please tick the box ☐

General Practitioner details:

Please state who recommended your child for physiotherapy:

___

1. Please give names and ages of any other brothers or sisters.

---

2. Please give a brief medical history and what age your child reached his/her milestones (e.g. sitting, crawling, standing and walking).

Sitting: **Crawling:**

Standing: **Walking:**

Did your child have a normal delivery?

Other relevant medical information (i.e. allergies, asthma, and other conditions):

- Does your child wear glasses?

- Has your child had an eye test? If yes, can you please state when and where.

---

3. What help if any, has your child received and was this intervention helpful?

---

4. What problems does your child have that you are concerned about?

---

5. What do you see are your child's main strengths?

---

6. Can your child

   a) ride a bicycle without stabilisers?

   b) dress him/herself?

   c) eat with a knife and fork?

   If your child has difficulty please explain.

---

7. Does your child have difficulty with writing, drawing and reading?
   Please elaborate:

---

8. What areas would you like to see improved through physiotherapy?

I agree for (name) to be assessed and relevant physiotherapy treatment given.

I also agree that information concerning my child may be used anonymously for research purposes only.

Consenting parent's signature: **Date:**

______________________________ _______________

Please see attached sheet relating to Consenting Advice *for parents*.

PARENTAL RESPONSIBILITY – CONSENTING ADVICE

The *Children Act 1989* sets out who has parental responsibility and these include:

- the child's parents if married to each other at the time of conception or birth;
- the child's mother, but not father if they were not so married *unless* the father has acquired parental responsibility via a court order or a parental responsibility agreement or the couple subsequently marry;
- the child's legally appointed guardian – appointed either by a court or by a parent with parental responsibility in the event of their own death;
- a person in whose favour a court has made a residence order concerning the child;
- a local authority designated in a care order in respect of the child (but not where the child is being looked after under section 20 of the *Children Act*, also known as being 'accommodated' or in 'voluntary care');
- a local authority or other authorised person who holds an emergency protection order in respect of the child.

The above text has been taken from *Seeking Consent: Working with Children* published by the Department of Health (2001).

QUESTIONNAIRE FOR SCHOOLS

Dear Class Teacher

We would be grateful if you could please answer the following questions to enable us to have a clear understanding of the child's present difficulties. When completed can you please either return this form to the parents or post directly to the Department at the above address.

Thank you.

1. Is the child happy at school? Please elaborate:
2. Where does the child sit in the classroom? Is this by choice or direction?
3. Does the child have difficulty copying or carrying out instructions?
4. Does the child tend to fidget excessively in class or during particular subjects?
5. Does the child easily lose concentration or become easily distracted?
6. Does the child have any extra support in the classroom?
7. Is the SENCO involved with the child?
8. Does the child have difficulty organising him/herself?
9. Is the child's work messy?
10. Does the child have difficulty with PE/games including getting changed?
11. What subject(s) does the child like/dislike at school?
12. Have you or has any other teacher implemented strategies to assist the child? If so, are these helpful?
13. Does the child form good relationships with his/her peer group?
14. Does the school have any other concerns? Please elaborate:

Teacher's signature:____________________________ **Date:**__________________

QUESTIONNAIRE FOR CHILD

Dear ______________________________

We are looking forward to seeing you on ___________________________

Please could you help us by answering these few questions (you could ask Mum or Dad to help you with this).

1. What do you enjoy doing at school?

2. What do you dislike at school?

3. What are your hobbies?

4. What extra activities do you do out of school?

5. Who do you play with at break time?

6. What games do you play at break time?

7. Please draw a picture of yourself.

Don't forget to bring your shorts and T-shirt to change into.

Thank you.

Appendix 3: Treatment Sheet

EXAMPLE OF RECORD SHEET

Name:

	Week 1	*Week 2*	*Week 3*	*Week 4*	*Week 5*	*Week 6*	*Week 7*
BACK EXTENSION							
Superman throwing balls							
The cannon							
Throwing the ball							
SHOULDER CONTROL							
Bunny hops							
Fruit picking							
Crabs							
Whizz ball							
Dog's dinner							
Moving the bean bag							
Traffic controller							
PELVIC CONTROL							
Bridging							
Scissors							
Step-ups							
Shoe shops							
Standing on one leg							
Kneel walking							
EQUIPMENT TAKEN							
SIGNED: **Date:**	Home Box						

Eye/Hand Co-ordination Activities:

Eye/Foot Co-ordination Activities:

Mini Trampoline Activities:

Scooter Board Activities:

Therapy Activities:

Memory Activities:

Planning Activities:

Hand Exercises:

Other Activities:

S:
O:
A:
P:

S: Subjective O: Objective A: Assessment P: Plan

Signed: ______________________ **Date:** ____________________

Appendix 4: Case Study

Name: James
Age: 6 years 5 months

James was referred for physiotherapy by a consultant paediatrician who had given a diagnosis of dyspraxia. There were general concerns about his co-ordination and writing skills.

General history

James was born by vaginal delivery at term following a normal pregnancy. He is the elder child of two and has a younger brother aged 4. He had several ear infections between the ages of 2 and 4 years and grommets were inserted at the age of 5. He was reported to have reached his milestones at the following times:

- sitting: 8–9 months
- crawling: did not
- standing: 11 months
- walking: 14 months

James was reported to have been late speaking (mother reported he did not really begin to talk before the age of 2½ years) and received speech therapy with good effect.

Parents' main concerns

- Poor writing.
- Poor ability to catch balls in comparison with younger brother and peers.
- Unable to use a knife properly.
- Slow at running.
- Looks awkward when climbing (climbing frames).

Class teacher's main concerns

- Poor concentration in class and never seems to sit still.
- Poor writing as he presses down heavily and is very slow.
- Finds games and PE difficult and shows poor co-ordination skills.
- Has difficulty remembering instructions and copying.

General impression

James presented as a friendly boy who was very co-operative and willing to attempt all activities asked of him. His concentration skills appeared poor and he would lose concentration easily, especially when attempting tasks he found difficult such as catching balls. Self-confidence appeared normal and when tested using the B/G Steem test he scored 14 points, which is considered at the lower range of normal. James informed the therapist of the following:

likes at school:	drama and listening to stories
dislikes at school:	writing and having school dinners
hobbies at home:	listening to pop music, playing on the computer
outside activities:	drama and swimming

The assessment

All areas were assessed and, in summary, the assessment revealed the following areas of difficulties:

Poor shoulder control

James was only able to complete 25 steps of wheelbarrows and, when carrying out the task, he did so with his hands landing heavily on the ground, a flexed posture and his pelvis swaying side to side.

Poor pelvic control

James was able to stand on the right leg for only six seconds and on the left for ten seconds. In addition, when walking backwards on his knees, he did so with a great deal of circumduction of the hips and he lost his balance easily in half kneeling. He was able to hop forwards 30 times on the right but only managed six times on the left.

Poor active trunk extension and flexion

James was able to hold the position of an aeroplane for only three seconds and a curled-up ball for only four seconds.

Poor eye/hand co-ordination

James was able to catch a football when thrown to him well but he had difficulty catching the ball when he threw it to himself with both hands and his dominant hand (right). He achieved only three out of five times for both tasks. When James used a tennis ball he was able to catch the ball only with two hands and could not throw and catch or bounce and catch the ball to himself with one hand.

Poor eye/foot co-ordination

James kicked a ball with poor direction and force and he was only able to trap a kicked ball with either foot two out of five times.

Poor midline crossing

When James took a bean bag from one side to the other with one hand, he did so either by throwing the bean bag from the midline position or by swapping hands at midline position.

Poor motor planning

When James climbed over four chairs he was very hesitant and crawled over them. When he climbed down, he was anxious and came down backwards.

Poor self-organisational skills

James was asked to make his favourite sandwich – ham and cheese. He managed only three sequences verbally and he demonstrated three sequences:
Verbal: 'Get two pieces of bread, put butter on them and then ham and cheese.'
Demonstrating: Two pieces of bread were taken out of a box, ham and cheese placed on one slice and the other slice placed on top.

Poor short-term memory

When James was given three tasks both visually and verbally he was only able to complete two out of three correctly.

Poor symmetrical integration

James was able to jump with both feet together forwards only five out of ten times.

Poor bilateral integration

James was able to complete only 15 alternate taps with foot and finger on the same side in 30 seconds, as opposed to the 30 that would be expected for his age group.

The treatment

An eight-week course of treatment was recommended consisting of weekly treatments supplemented by a daily home programme.

The short-term plan of treatment

- Teach James and his parents the daily home programme.
- Liaise with the school by sending, via the parents, a liaison diary, a booklet with advice on how to help James in the classroom and in the games situation.

The long-term plan of treatment

- Improve shoulder control so that, by the review, James could complete 70–100 steps of wheelbarrows with no trunk flexion or swaying of the hips.
- Improve pelvic control so that, by the review, James could stand on either leg for 15–20 seconds and could walk backwards on his knees without circumducting the hips, and could maintain a half-kneeling position with improved balance.
- Improve active trunk extension and flexion so that, by the review, James could maintain the position of an aeroplane for 10–15 seconds and maintain the position of a curl-up for 10–15 seconds.
- Improve eye/hand co-ordination so that, by the review, James could throw and catch a tennis ball to himself with his dominant hand five out of five times.
- Improve eye/foot co-ordination so that, by the review, James could kick a ball with good force and direction and trap a kicked ball with either leg five out of five times.
- Improve motor planning so that, by the review, James could climb over the chairs with ease.
- Improve self-organisational skills so that, by the review, James could verbalise, and demonstrate, making a sandwich with 6+ sequences.
- Improve midline crossing so that, by the review, James could take a bean bag from one side and place it on his other side using the same hand five out of five times.
- Improve short-term memory so that, by the review, James could carry out a sequence of 3–4 activities when shown and asked.

- Improve symmetrical integration so that, by the review, James could jump forwards with both feet landing together ten out of ten times.
- Improve bilateral integration so that, by the review, James could carry out the task of alternate tapping one foot and hand on the same side 25–30 times in 30 seconds.

Goals set with James and his parents

- To improve James' ability to use a knife and fork.
- To improve James' speed and style of running.
- To improve James' writing ability.
- To improve James' ability to catch a ball 'so that he could catch like his friends'.

Treatment plan week by week

Session 1

Home programme taught showing activities for shoulder control, pelvic control and active trunk extension.

Parents advised to complete three shoulder, three hip and one back exercise daily.

Ball games:	Using a bean bag throw and catch to person. Throw and catch to self using the right hand (dominant). Batting a balloon to self.

Parents advised to continue ball games at home with ten repetitions only.

Trampoline:	Jump up and down ten times, jump astride ten times and throw a football to therapist and catch it ten times while continuing to jump.
Large therapy ball:	Throw and catch to a person using two hands. Sitting on it – try to take child off balance.
Games for co-ordination:	Labyrinth game – with first plate Springy Spiders Magnetic fishing game
Memory:	Button Maze (also helps with eye/hand co-ordination and midline crossing)
Game lent for week:	Button Maze

Session 2

Home programme checked and ensured that parents and child were completing it correctly with no difficulties.

Exercises increased to 15 repetitions for each exercise.

Ball games:	As before but using a juggling ball only.

Ball games to be done at home with ten repetitions.

Trampoline:	As above but with 20 jumps.
Large therapy ball:	As above.
Games for co-ordination:	Labyrinth – with first plate Buzzy Bees
Memory game:	Speedy Fingers
Bilateral integration:	Using a scooter and moving in and out of cones.
Game lent for week:	Buzzy Bees

Session 3

Home programme checked and ensured that parents and child were completing it correctly with no difficulties.

Exercises increased to 20 repetitions for each exercise.

Ball games:	As before but using a tennis ball only

Ball games to be done at home with ten repetitions.

Trampoline:	As above but with 25 jumps.
Large therapy ball:	As above.
Games for co-ordination:	Labyrinth – with second plate Magna Force Magnetic Maze
Memory/motor planning:	Obstacle course with six items: go through tunnel, bounce on space hopper around cones, stand on Sissel cushion and throw ten bean bags into box, walk on stilts around cones, climb over six chairs and do hop scotch in and out of hoops. Course then completed reversed. Obstacle course changed with another six items.
Game lent for week:	Speedy Fingers

Session 4

Home programme checked and ensured that parents and child were completing it correctly with no difficulties.

Exercises increased to 25 repetitions for each exercise.

Ball games:	Tennis ball thrown in air with two hands and caught and bounced and caught to self using two hands.

Ball games to be done at home with ten repetitions.

Trampoline:	As above but with 25 jumps.
Large therapy ball:	As above.
Games for co-ordination:	Labyrinth – with second plate Magna Force Kick a ball to knock down skittles
Memory/motor planning:	Obstacle course with seven items: walk on stilts around cones, with scooter board go in and out of cones, crab walk in and out of cones, go through tunnel, jump ten times forwards, bounce tennis ball on the wall and catch again five times and hop to end of room. Course then completed reversed. Obstacle course changed with another seven items.
Game lent for week:	Magna Force

Session 5

Checked scores for shoulder control:	70 steps
pelvic control:	right leg: 15 seconds
	left leg: 20 seconds
active trunk extension:	15 seconds
Home programme 2	Taught with change of compulsory exercises which were varied on alternate days.
Exercises:	Two shoulder, two hip and one back exercises to be completed at home with 30 repetitions. Whizz ball used for shoulder control exercise. Two hand exercises with the right hand to be carried out at home with ten repetitions. To make a job list of daily chores and to tick off daily and bring back next week completed for a sticker. To verbally recall journey from home to school making a note of landmarks and where to turn into specific roads.
Ball games:	Throw tennis ball into the air with two hands, touch tummy with two hands and catch. Bounce ball, touch tummy with two hands before catching ball using a bat and Koosh, bat to himself with as many repetitions as possible.

Ball games to be done at home with ten repetitions.

Trampoline:	As above but with 30 jumps.
Large therapy ball:	As above.
Games for co-ordination:	Greedy Frogs Kick ball under chair and into goal Walk on stilts onto specific spots Big Foot game
Games for organisational skills:	Go Getter 1 Rush Hour
Games lent for week:	Rush Hour and Go Getter 1

Session 6

Home programme checked and ensured that parents and were child completing it correctly with no difficulties.

Exercises increased to 35 repetitions for each exercise but hand exercises to remain at ten. Star given for completing daily job list.

Ball games:	Tennis ball – throw in air with right (dominant) hand only and catch. As above but bounce ball and catch. As above but with touching tummy before catching.

Ball games to be done at home with ten repetitions.

Trampoline:	As above but with 35 jumps.
Large therapy ball:	As above.

Games for co-ordination:	Air hockey Kicking ball to knock down skittles
Memory/motor planning:	Obstacle course with eight items: go through tunnel, walk on stilts in and out of cones, jump into and out of six hoops, stand on Sissel cushion and throw ten bean bags into box, throw tennis ball against wall, clap hands and catch with two hands five times, kick ball around cones and then kick ball into goal, crab walk in and out of cones, walk backwards on knees back to the beginning point. Course then completed reversed.
Games for self-organisation:	Go Getter 2 Downfall To highlight route on map from one town to another
Game lent for week:	Downfall

Session 7

Home programme checked and ensured that parents and child were completing it correctly with no difficulties.

Exercises increased to 40 repetitions for each exercise but hand exercises to remain at ten. Star given for completing jobs daily.

Ball games:	Tennis ball thrown in air with right (dominant) hand only, touch head and catch.

As above but bounce ball, touch head and catch.

Ball games to be done at home with ten repetitions.

Trampoline:	As above but with 35 jumps.
Large therapy ball:	As above.
Games for co-ordination:	Pick-up sticks Buzz Off
Games for self-organisation:	Hopper Marble Maze As James is going away for the weekend to stay with grandparents, he will write out list of things he needs to take with him and then pack his own bag.
Game lent for week:	Pick-up sticks and Hopper

Session 8

Checklist completed with the following scores obtained:

Shoulder control:	92 steps of wheelbarrows
Pelvic control:	stand on right leg: 22 seconds stand on left leg: 20 seconds hops forward right leg: 55 hops forward left leg: 25
Active trunk extension:	aeroplane: 20 seconds
Active trunk flexion:	curled-up ball: 22 seconds

Symmetrical integration:	jumps forwards: 10 out of 10 – both feet landed together jumping jack: 10 out of 10
Ball skills:	– able to catch a tennis ball when thrown to both hands and to either hand five out of five times. – able to catch a tennis ball when thrown to self with both hands and with either hand five out of five times. – able to bounce a tennis ball and catch to self with two hands and with either hand five out of five times.
Kicking skill:	Good force and direction. Stopped a trapped ball five out of five times.
Bilateral integration:	25 taps in 30 seconds.
Midline crossing:	Able to take a bean bag from one side of body to the other with one hand five out of five times.
Motor planning:	Able to climb over four chairs with ease and get down from last chair forwards.
Self-organisation:	Able to verbally quote seven sequences; get a plate and knife out, get butter, ham and cheese out of fridge, spread the butter with a knife, put the ham on next followed by the cheese, put the other bread on top, and then eat it.

School report

The class teacher had completed the liaison diary fortnightly and reported for the last session that James' writing was improving tremendously and that he was beginning to sit for longer periods and concentrate. He still had difficulty with remembering instructions although this was improving, especially when she gave a maximum of only three instructions and asked James to repeat them to her before carrying them out.

Plan of action until the review

For the first six weeks:

- To continue with two shoulder, two hip and one back extension exercise (varying exercises weekly) with 40 repetitions on alternate days.
- To continue with memory activities on alternate days.
- To continue with ball games of throwing and catching a tennis ball to himself, touching head, tummy and then catching with right hand. As above, but with bounce and catch and throw against wall and catch. Ten repetitions alternate days.
- To continue with self-organisational skills, using tick-off chart job list, encourage map reading, cooking and packing items for school, swimming sessions, etc.
- As the family had a small trampoline in the garden, James was encouraged to use this instead of one of the pelvic control exercises (provided adequate supervision was given) and to use the scooter at home.

For the last six weeks until review:

- Continue with the above programme but only twice a week.
- During this time, James was encouraged to carry out some more hobbies and activities. He already swam once a week and had shown an interest in doing judo, short tennis and football. It was recommended that he should carry out no more than two outside activities

The review three months following treatment

General update

James had continued with the treatment plan but, since returning to school three weeks ago, he had continued with the programme only once a week.

Parents' comments

- Writing had improved and James had received a good school report.
- He was joining in all ball games with his friends now.
- He was not such a messy eater and could generally cut up all food.
- He was quicker at running and could now keep up with his younger brother.
- James was more willing to go on climbing frames but occasionally still looked awkward.

Class teacher's comments

- Concentration was reported to be generally better in class but, if a task was difficult, he would fidget and move around the classroom.
- Writing had improved and he was a lot quicker.
- James was finding games and PE lessons more enjoyable and could catch balls well now.
- Generally James was able to remember instructions but he needed to be asked to repeat them before he carried them out.

General impression at review

James presented as a very friendly boy who was very co-operative and willing to attempt all activities asked of him. His concentration skills appeared greatly improved and he did not lose his concentration during the assessment. Self-confidence appeared good and, on testing, James (using the B/G Steem test) scored 18 points which is considered to be high. James informed the therapist of the following:

Likes at school:	drama, games, English
Dislikes at school:	having school dinners
Hobbies at home:	playing football in the garden, playing on the computer, riding his bicycle
Outside activities:	drama, judo and swimming

The review assessment

All areas were assessed and in summary the assessment revealed the following improvements:

Shoulder control

James was now able to do 102 steps of wheelbarrows as opposed to 25 steps at the initial assessment. He could now complete the task with his hands landing softly on the ground, more extended posture and his pelvis no longer swayed side to side.

Pelvic control

James was now able to stand on the right and left legs for 25 seconds as opposed to initially standing on the right leg for six seconds and on the left for ten seconds. In addition, he could now walk on his knees backwards with only minimal circumduction of the hips and he no longer lost his balance easily in half kneeling. He could now hop 50 times on the right foot as opposed to 30 times and on the left 30 times instead of six times.

Active trunk extension and flexion

James was now able to hold the position of an aeroplane for 22 seconds as opposed to six seconds and a curled-up ball for 22 seconds as opposed to four seconds.

Eye/hand co-ordination

James was now able to achieve all ball activities five out of five times and he could also, when throwing and catching to himself, clap his hands before catching a tennis ball with his right hand five out of five times.

Eye/foot co-ordination

James was now able to kick a ball with good direction and force and was able to trap a kicked ball with either foot five out of five times.

Midline crossing

James was able to take bean bags from one side to the other with one hand correctly five out of five times

Motor planning

James was able to climb over four chairs with less hesitancy and showed less anxiety when he climbed off the chairs, which he could do by coming off the chairs forwards instead of backwards as he had done initially.

Self-organisational skills

James was able to verbally state and demonstrate seven sequences about making a cheese and ham sandwich. This was stated as: 'Get two pieces of bread. Place the bread on a plate. Butter one side of both pieces of bread. Get the cheese and ham out of the fridge and place on one of the slices of bread. Put the other slice of bread on top and then eat it.' James then demonstrated this.

Short-term memory

James was able to complete three tasks both visually and verbally and could also verbally carry out four tasks when asked of him.

Symmetrical integration

James was able to jump with both feet together forwards and also now backwards ten out of ten times as opposed to five out of ten times.

Bilateral integration

James was able to complete 26 alternate taps with foot and finger on the same side in 30 seconds as opposed to 15.

Summary

From the scores taken and using the outcome measures, James showed an improvement with his gross motor skills of 72 per cent. His mother also reported an improvement of 75 per cent with the activities that she had wanted to see improved. James was encouraged to continue with his outside activities, playing ball games, practising climbing on frames and visiting adventure playgrounds. His parents were given a checklist of activities to complete monthly to ensure that his scores remained at a similar level to those at the review and he was to be reviewed in one year.

Annual review

James was reviewed one year later and it was reported that there were no difficulties apart from remembering what homework he had been given. There were no other current concerns either at home or at school. All his scores remained at the improved level from his last review and James had received a very good end of school year report. He won an award for effort at school. His parents and class teacher were advised to give James a homework book so that he could write down his homework. This was then to be checked daily by the class teacher. James was also encouraged to write a homework timetable for home so that both he and his mother knew which homework subjects he had each night. The family were also given an updated checklist to continue with on a monthly basis and it was agreed that annual reviews would continue at least until he started secondary school. In addition, leaflets for the school were given to the new class teacher.

Resources

Useful addresses

Ann Arbor Publishing
PO Box 1
Belford
Northumberland NE70 7JX
Tel: 01668 214460
Fax: 01668 214484
www.annarbor.co.uk

Dyspraxia Foundation
8 West Alley
Hitchin
Herts SG5 1ED
Tel: 01462 454986

Lucky Duck Publishing Ltd
Solar House
Station Road
Kingswood
Bristol BS15 4PH
Tel: 0117 947 5150
Fax: 0117 947 5152
www.luckyduck.co.uk

Multistage Fitness Test
National Coaching Foundation
114 Cardigan Road
Headingley
Leeds LS6 3BJ
Tel: 0113 275 5019

NFER-Nelson
The Chiswick Centre
414 Chiswick High Road
London W4 5TF
Tel: 0208 996 8444
Fax: 0208 996 3660
www.nfer-nelson.co.uk

Suppliers of equipment and games to assist dyspraxia/DCD

Back in Action
11 Whitcomb Street
Trafalgar Square
London WC2H 7HA
Tel: 020 7930 8309
Fax: 020 7925 0250
www.backinaction.co.uk

The Happy Puzzle Company
Hill House
Highgate Hill
London N19 5UU
Tel: 0800 376 3728
www.happypuzzle.co.uk

Nottingham Rehab Supplies
Findel House
Excelsior Road
Ashby Park
Ashby de la Zouch
Leics LE65 1NG
Tel: 0115 923 5264
www.nrs-uk.co.uk

OT ideas Inc
www.otideas.com

Philip & Tacey Ltd
North Way
Andover
Hants SP10 5BA
Tel: 01264 332171
Fax: 01264 384808
www.philipandtacey.co.uk

Physio Med Services
7–23 Glossop Brook Business Park
Surrey Street
Glossop
Derbyshire SK13 7AJ
Tel: 01457 860 444
www.physio-med.com

Psychological Corporation
32 Jamestown Road
London NW1 7BY
Tel: 0207 424 4456
www.harcourt-uk.com

Rompa International
Goyt Side Road
Chesterfield
Derbyshire S40 2PH
Tel: 0800 056 2323
www.rompa.com

Sissal UK Ltd
10 Moderna Business Park
Mytholmroyd
Halifax
West Yorkshire HX7 5RH
Tel: 01422 885433

Taskmaster
Morris Road
Leicester LE2 6BR
Tel: 0116 270 4286
Fax: 0116 270 6992
www.taskmasteronline.co.uk

Bibliography

Addy, L. (1996) 'A multi-professional approach to the treatment of developmental coordination disorder', *British Journal of Therapy and Rehabilitation* **3**(11): 593–9.

Alston, J. and Taylor, J. (1984) *The Handwriting File: Diagnosis and Remediation of Handwriting Difficulties*, Wisbech: Learning Development Aids.

American Psychiatric Association (1994) *Diagnostic and Statistical Manual of Mental Disorders*. DSM IV International version with ICD-10 codes. Washington, DC: American Psychiatric Association.

Association of Paediatric Chartered Physiotherapists (1997) *Statutory Assessment of Children with Special Educational Needs: Guidelines for Paediatric Physiotherapists and Other Professionals*. London: Chartered Society of Physiotherapy.

Ayres, A. J. (1972) *Sensory Integration and Learning Disorders*. Los Angeles, CA: Western Psychological Services.

Ayres, A. J. (1979) *Sensory Integration and the Child*. Los Angeles, CA: Western Psychological Services.

Baker, J. (1981) 'A psycho-motor approach to the assessment and treatment of clumsy children', *Physiotherapy* **67**(12): 356–63.

Bayley N. (1969) *Manual for the Bayley Scale of Infant Development*. Berkeley, CA: The Psychological Corporation.

Bobath, B. and Bobath, K. (1975) *Motor Development in the Different Kinds of Cerebral Palsy*. London: Heinemann.

Cermak, S. (1991) 'Motorsensory dyspraxia', in A. Fisher, E. A. Murray and A. C. Bundy (eds), *Sensory Integration: Theory and Practice*. Philadelphia: F. A. Davis, 138–70.

Chu, S. (1998) 'Developmental dyspraxia 1: the diagnosis', *British Journal of Therapy and Rehabilitation* **5**(3): 131–8.

Cocks, N. (1996) *Watch Me, I Can Do It! Helping Children Overcome Clumsy and Uncoordinated Motor Skill*. East Roseville, NSW: Simon & Schuster.

College of Occupational Therapists, National Association of Paediatric Occupational Therapists (2003) *Children with Developmental Coordination Disorder: Report on a Survey of Waiting Lists and Waiting Times for Occupational Therapy Services for Children with Developmental Coordination Disorder*. London: College of Occupational Therapists.

Colley, M. (2000) *Living with Dyspraxia: A Guide for Adults with Developmental Dyspraxia*. Hitchin: Dyspraxia Foundation Adult Support Group.

Denckla, M. B., Rudel, R. G., Chapman, C. and Kreiger, J. (1985) 'Motor proficiency in dyslexic children: theoretical and clinical implications', in F. H. Duffy and N. Geschwind (eds), *Dyslexia: A Neuroscientific Approach to Clinical Evaluations*. Boston, MA: Little Brown, 182–205.

Department of Health (2001) *Seeking Consent: Working with Children*.

Dyspraxia Foundation (1990) *Developmental Dyspraxia Explained*. Hitchin: Dyspraxia Foundation.

Dyspraxia Foundation (1997) *Member's Questionnaire 1997. Awareness and Diagnosis*. Hitchin: Dyspraxia Foundation.

Edelman, G. M. (1989) *Neural Darwinism: The Theory of Neuronal Group Selection.* Oxford: Oxford University Press.

Fink, B. (1989) *Sensory-Motor Integration Activities.* Tucson, AZ: Therapy Skill Builders.

Fog, E. and Fog, M. (1963) 'Cerebral inhibition examined by associated movements', in R. MacKeith and M. Bax (eds), *Minimal Cerebral Dysfunction.* Clinics in Developmental Medicine No. 10. London: Heinemann.

French, J. and Patterson, M. (1992) 'The psychological development of the child: its implications for physiotherapy practice', in S. French (ed.), *Physiotherapy: A Psycho Social Approach.* London: Butterworth Heinemann, 256–72.

Frostig, M. and Horne, D. (1964) *The Frostig Programme for the Development of Visual Perception.* Chicago, IL: Follet Publishing Company.

Geuze, R. H., Jongmans, M. J., Schoemaker, M. M. and Smits-Engelsman, B. C. (2001) 'Clinical and research diagnostic criteria for developmental coordination disorder: a review and discussion', *Human Movement Science* **20**(12): 7–47.

Glendenning, K., Ryan, A. and Fonseca, J. (2003) 'Improving motor skills and learning skills in dyspraxic children by improving postural base, stability and visual-motor control: a pilot study', *Association of Paediatric Chartered Physiotherapists* **109**: 9–21.

Goddard-Blyth, S. A. and Hyland, D. (1998) 'Screening for neurophysiological dysfunction in the specific learning difficulty child', *British Journal of Occupational Therapy* **61**(10): 459–64.

Gordon, N. and McKinlay, I. (1980) *Helping Clumsy Children.* Edinburgh: Churchill Livingstone.

Griffiths, R. (1970) *The Abilities of the Young Child.* London: Child Development Research Centre.

Grimley, A. and Gordon, N. (1977) *The Clumsy Child* (an APCP publication). London: Chartered Society of Physiotherapy.

Gubbay, S. S. (1975a) *The Clumsy Child: A Study of Developmental Apraxia and Agnosia.* London: W. B. Saunders.

Gubbay, S. S. (1975b) 'Clumsy children in normal schools', *Medical Journal of Australia* **1**: 223–6.

Gubbay, S. S. (1985) in P. J. Vinken, G. W. Bruyn and H. L. Klawans (eds), *Clumsiness: Handbook of Clinician Neurology.* New York: Elsevier, pp. 159–67

Hall, D., Hill, P. and Elliman, D. (1991) *The Child Surveillance Handbook.* Oxford: Radcliffe Medical Press.

Hall, E. (1995) *Learning Disabilities and the American Public: A Look at American Awareness and Knowledge.* Tremain Foundation/Roper Starch Worldwide National Poll.

Henderson, S. E. and Sugden, D. (1992) *Movement Assessment Battery for Children.* New York: Harcourt Brace/The Psychological Corporation.

Henderson, S. E. and Hall, D. (1982) 'Concomitants of clumsiness in young school children', *Developmental Medicine and Child Neurology* **24**: 448–60.

Kadesjo, B. and Gillberg, C. (2001) 'The comorbidity of ADHD in the general population of Swedish school age children', *Journal of Child Psychology and Psychiatry* **42**: 487–92.

Kaplan, B. J., Wilson, B. N., Dewey, D. and Crawford, S. G. (1998) 'DCD may not be a discrete disorder', *Human Movement Science* **17**: 471–90.

Kephart, N. C. (1960) *The Slow Learner in the Classroom.* Columbus, OH: Charles E. Merrill Publishers.

Kiphard, E. J. and Schilling, F. (1974) *The Body Coordination Test.* Weinhem: Belz Test Gmbh.

Kohen-Raz, R. (1986) *Learning Difficulties and Postural Control.* London: Freund.

Laszlo, J. L. and Bairstow, P. L. (1985) *Perceptual Motor Behaviour, Developmental Assessment and Therapy.* Eastbourne: Holt Rinehart and Winston.

Lee, M. G. (1998) 'Dyspraxia and the importance of self confidence and self esteem', *British Journal of Therapy and Rehabilitation* **5**(10): 500–1.

Lee, M. G. (2000) *Setting Up a Dyspraxia Physiotherapy Service* (2nd edn) (obtainable from the Lee Medical Practice, Blaire House, Denham Green Lane, Denham, Bucks UB9 5LQ).

Lee, M. G. and French, J. (1994) *Dyspraxia: A Handbook for Therapists*. London: Association of Paediatric Chartered Physiotherapists, Chartered Society of Physiotherapy.

Lee, M. G. and Gronmark, J. (2000) *Ages Children with Dyspraxia Reach Their Milestones*. Proceedings from Conference 2000. Hitchin: Dyspraxia Foundation.

Lee, M. G. and Smith, G. N. (1998) 'The effectiveness of physiotherapy for dyspraxia', *Physiotherapy* **84**(6): 276–84.

Lee, M. G. and Smith, G. N. (2002) 'A three year study on the progress of children following physiotherapy treatment for dyspraxia', *Dyspraxia Foundation Professional Journal* **1**: 9–23.

Lee, M. G. and Yoxall, S. (2004) *Changes in Interests Following Physiotherapy Treatment for Children with Dyspraxia*. Poster presentation at DCD Conference, Oxford.

Lee, M. G., Yoxall, S. and Smith, P. (2003) 'The improvement made with self esteem following physiotherapy treatment for dyspraxia', *Dyspraxia Foundation Professional Journal* **2**: 44–8.

Lerner, J. (1985) *Learning Disabilities* (4th edn). Boston, MA: Houghton Mifflin Company.

Macintyre, C. (2000) *Dyspraxia in the Early Years*. London: David Fulton.

Miller, L. (1989) *The Miller Assessment for Preschoolers*. London: The Psychological Corporation.

Miller, L. (1993a) *First Steps*. London: The Psychological Corporation.

Miller, L. (1993b) *ITSE*. London: The Psychological Corporation.

Missiuna, C. and Polatajko, H. (1995) 'Developmental dyspraxia by any other name: are they all just clumsy children?' *American Journal of Occupational Therapy* **49**: 619–27.

Mitchell, D. and Wood, N. (1999) 'An investigation of midline crossing in 3 year old children', *Physiotherapy* **85**(11): 613–21.

Myers, S. (2002) *Assessing the Effects of a Daily Structured Motor Skills Programme on the Attainments, Concentration and Self Esteem in a Group Key Stage 1 Pupils' Special Study*. Durham: University of Durham.

Norton, J. and Twentyman, H. (1995) 'Group therapy for children with coordination problems', *Association of Paediatric Chartered Physiotherapists* **75**: 32–6.

Oliver, C. (1990) 'A sensorimotor program for improving writing readiness skills in elementary-aged children', *American Journal of Occupational Therapy* **44**(2): 111–16.

Polatajko, H. J., Fox, M. and Missiuna, C. (1995) 'An international consensus on children with developmental coordination disorder', *Canadian Journal of Occupational Therapy* **62**: 3–6.

Portwood, M. M. (1999) *Developmental Dyspraxia, Identification and Intervention: A Manual for Parents and Professionals* (2nd edn). London: David Fulton.

Portwood, M. M. (2000) *Understanding Developmental Dyspraxia: A Textbook for Students and Professionals*. London: David Fulton.

Portwood, M. M. (2003) *Dyslexia and PE*. London: David Fulton.

Portwood, M. M. (2004) 'Dyspraxia', in A. Lewis and B. Norwich (eds), *Special Teaching for Special Children*. Maidenhead: Open University Press.

Quigg, J. (2003) 'Effectiveness of group work for children with learning disabilities', *British Journal of Therapy and Rehabilitation* **10**(1): 29–33.

Ramus, F., Pidgeon, E. and Frith, U. (2003) 'The relationship between motor control and phonology in dyslexic children', *Journal of Child Psychology and Psychiatry and Allied Disciplines* **44**: 712–22.

Russell, J. (1988) *Graded Activities for Children with Motor Difficulties*. Cambridge: Cambridge University Press.

Sasson, R. (1990) *Handwriting: A New Perspective*. London: Stanley Thornes.

Sherbourne, V. (1990) *Developmental Movement for Children*. Cambridge: Cambridge University Press.

Sheridan, M. D. (1975) *From Birth to Five Years*. Windsor: NFER-Nelson.

Sheridan, M. D. (1997) *From Birth to Five Years: Children's Developmental Progress*. London: Routledge.

Silver, L. B. (1991) *The Misunderstood Child*. Blue Ridge Summit, PA: Tab Books.

Stott, D. H., Moyes, F. A. and Henderson, S. E. (1984a) 'Clumsy children: a study of developmental apraxia and agnosia', *Brain* **85**: 603–13.

Stott, D. H., Moyes, F. A. and Henderson, S. E. (1984b) *Test of Motor Impairment.* Guelph, Ont.: Brook Educational Ltd.

Sugden, D. A. and Chambers, M. E. (1998) 'Intervention approaches and children with developmental coordination disorder', *Paediatric Rehabilitation* **2**(4): 139–47.

Sugden, D. A. and Keogh, J. F. (1990) *Problems in Movement Skill Development.* Columbia, SC: University of South Carolina.

Thelen, E. (1989) 'The (re) discovery of motor development: learning new things from an old field', *Developmental Psychology* **25**: 946–9.

Wetton, P. (1997) *Physical Education in the Early Years.* London: Routledge.

Williams, C. A., Smith, J. and Ainsley, J. (1999) 'The effects of a physiotherapy intervention programme on children with developmental coordination disorder', *Association of Paediatric Chartered Physiotherapists* **91**: 32–40.

Wimmer, H., Mayringer, H. and Landerl, K. (1998) 'Poor reading: a deficit in skill-automatization or a poor phonological deficit?' *Scientific Studies of Reading* **2**(4): 321–40.

Wolff, P. H. (1999) 'A candidate phenotype for familial dyslexia', *European Child and Adolescent Psychiatry* **8**(7): 5021–7.

Available from the Dyspraxia Foundation

Discover Yourself by Gill Dixon

Getting Extra Help, Advisory Centre for Education

Life Skills: Practical Solutions for Specific Learning Difficulties by Jan Poustie

Praxis Makes Perfect II (for teachers)

Take Time by Mary Nash-Wortham and Jean Hunt

Tips with Teens by Lillian Beattie

Index

Co-ordination Difficulties

Related titles of interest

Developmental Dyspraxia: Identification and Intervention (1999)
Madeleine Portwood (1-85346-573-9)

Understanding Developmental Dyspraxia: A Textbook for Students and Professionals (2000)
Madeleine Portwood (1-85346-574-7)

Dyspraxia: A Guide for Teachers and Parents (1997)
Kate Ripley, Bob Daines and Jenny Barrett (1-85346-444-9)

Guide to Dyspraxia and Developmental Co-ordination Disorders (2002)
Amanda Kirby and Sharon Drew (1-85346-913-0)

Inclusion for Children with Dyspraxia/DCD: A Handbook for Teachers (2001)
Kate Ripley (1-85346-762-6)